The Minister's Manual for Funerals

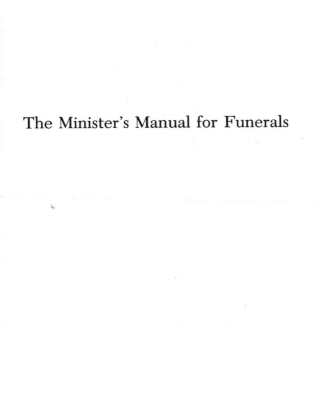

THE MINISTER'S MANUAL FOR FUNERALS

AL CADENHEAD, JR.

BROADMAN
& HOLMAN
PUBLISHERS

Nashville, Tennessee

© Copyright 1988 • Broadman Press
All Rights Reserved
4223-17
ISBN: 0-8054-2317-6

Dewey Decimal Classification: 252.1
Subject Heading: FUNERAL RITES AND CEREMONIES
Library of Congress Catalog Number: 87-14616

Printed in the United States of America

Unless otherwise stated, all Scripture quotations are from the *New King James Version.* Copyright © 1979, 1980, 1982, Thomas Nelson, Inc., Publishers.

Scripture quotations marked KJV are from the King James Version of the Bible.

Scripture quotations marked Moffatt are from *The Bible: a New Translation* by James A. R. Moffatt. Copyright © 1935 by Harper and Row, Publishers, Inc. Used by permission.

Library of Congress Cataloging-in-Publication Data

Cadenhead, Al, 1947-
Minister's manual for funerals.

    Bibliography: p.
        1. Funeral service—Handbooks, manuals, etc.
2. Funeral sermons.   3. Sermons, American.
I. Title.
BV199.F8C33   1988   265'.85   87-14616
ISBN 0-8054-2317-6

*Dedicated to those friends who,
in their dying, have taught us
lessons about living.*

Preface

The plans for this book began several years ago as I personally sought quality resources for my work with grieving families. With such an abundance of homeletical materials in general, I was concerned that there seemed to be very little to offer guidance for the funeral setting. The goal of this book is to provide resource material for a setting that has so much potential for ministry.

I am grateful to Broadman for their confidence in allowing this project to become a reality. I am also indebted to my family and my congregation at The Hill Baptist Church for their support during the months of preparation of these materials. A special thank you to my secretary, Mrs. Wyanne Hall, for many hours of turning my poor handwriting into a legible manuscript.

Contents

Introduction

The funeral setting provides an opportunity and a challenge for the minister. The entire experience is an opportunity to communicate the warmth of a loving God at a time of grief and pain. The funeral service itself is a challenge for the pastor to prepare comforting words of substance and integrity.

Entirely too often the pastor, due to a lack of personal preparation, falls back on words and expressions that are hollow and trite at a time when the griever is desperate for the depth of God's message. The minister has an unchallenged opportunity to embody God's love for the grieving family. The time is a critical one, but a perfect time to do what a pastor does best: minister.

Frequently, funerals come at a time when the minister is already working under the pressure of a crowded schedule. It is not uncommon to receive a last-minute request to officiate a funeral. Yet, time pressure does not do away with the need for substance when the minister stands before a grieving family. Preparation is a necessity.

The funeral setting is not only a time of offering comfort but can be an opportunity to build or strengthen a relationship with surviving members of the family. There will seldom be another setting where the relationship between minister and family will be more precious.

Therefore, the funeral setting is a time to be taken very seriously by the minister. This critical time is, indeed, a time of opportunity and challenge. Two elements become essential. There must first be a prayerful willingness to be used of God in a setting of great need. The minister becomes God's voice for the suffering family. Secondly, the prayerful willingness to be God's voice does not rule out the need for preparation. Particularly as the minister stands before the family in the service, he needs to have done his homework. Even God's instruments need to prepare.

The contents of this book are designed to guide the minister and offer assistance during a busy schedule. The materials are not to be used as a substitute for preparation. The goal is to provide additional resources to guide the minister's thoughts and actions during this crucial time in general and the funeral setting in particular.

1
Pastoral Care in the Grief Setting

Claiming the Role

Dr. Carlyle Marney once began a sermon by looking over his congregation and saying, "What a bunch of losers!"[1] In so doing he did not mean the usual understanding of a loser. Instead, he was alluding to the fact that for each of us, time eventually runs out. Not one is exempt. Sooner or later death breaks into our circles and we become persons of grief, acquainted with sorrow. In one sense we all really *are* a bunch of losers.

There will be few times in the life of a pastor when the potential for ministry will be greater than when death invades the ranks of a family. This time is an excellent opportunity for a pastor to approach a family from within a role that has two important elements.

The minister offers, first of all, himself. The gift of his presence, support, and encouragement is not to be valued lightly. Although the role carries with it certain expectations, the minister reaches out not just because he is expected to do so. He approaches the family because he cares and wants them to know it.

Secondly, as he moves toward that grieving family, more than just his own concern is communicated. As a minister he has the opportunity to provide an embodiment of Christ's love in a physical, tangible way. In a time of great need, the minister becomes a visible reminder of God's presence during these hours of pain.

In describing the symbolic role of the minister, Wayne Oates said, "The Christian pastor, then, is a representative of God, commissioned to bring the ruling sense of the presence of God to bear upon the conflict-weary lives of men and women."[2] There can be little debate that the death of a family member creates the conditions for a weary soul. The minister becomes an agent of help and healing because he carries with him more than his own personal presence. Never take for granted the mystery of the symbolic role of a minister.

Therefore, the pastor usually is very quickly and readily received in these circumstances. In very few circumstances will the symbolic role of the pastor be ignored or rejected. Even families who have never developed a strong relationship with their church or minister will frequently open themselves to the ministering spirit of their pastor.

There is also the opportunity for the development of a relationship that is unequaled in the normal routine of life. The potential exists for persons who have become church "dropouts" to be redeemed back into a productive relationship with the institutional church because of the care extended by the minister and church family during a time of grief. To ignore an opportunity for ministry so full of potential is tragic indeed.

In most cases the role of the minister is readily received by the grieving family. In many functions, the minister must slowly earn the authority granted him. In the context of personal loss, the role of the minister is usually granted by nature of his position in the local church. It is truly an opportunity to symbolize the warmth of a loving God at a time of need, even great pain. The place to begin for any minister is to claim this sacred role.

Guiding Principles

There are very few hard and fixed rules to follow when dealing with grieving families. However, a compassionate spirit and a little common sense go a long way.

Timely Response

There are some general principles that ministers should consider when ministering to a grieving family. Some of these are more within the realm of the practical than the theological. For example, it is important that the minister make a timely response to the grieving family. The message concerning the death will frequently interrupt the immediate plans of the minister. Depending upon circumstances one may not be able to contact the family immediately. However, be careful about indefinitely postponing a response. To make an assumption that the family knows you care is a dangerous proposition. Prompt response is crucial.

This response does not demand a siren and a race to the family. Yet, to wait for a long period of time before making contact may take on the appearance of unconcern, justifiable or not.

Do not be offended if the word comes to you indirectly. In many cases the family will contact you directly. In other circumstances an extended relative or friend may be the contact person for you. It very well may be the funeral director who notifies you of the death. Regardless of who tells you, you should immediately begin the process of making contact with the family.

A brief telephone call may suffice for the moment. This call to the family will accomplish several purposes. In so doing, you let the family know that you have received the word about the death. One of the many anxieties for a family during a death/crisis is the process of notifying relatives and friends. The family can relax that, at least, contact has been made with their minister.

If you do not plan to go to the family immediately, this call provides an opportunity to let them know when they can expect you. Your visit, in most cases, is important enough that a family will have interest in visiting privately. In some cases you will want to set a time very soon. In some cases a later time will be appropriate. A little common sense will be quite valuable at this point.

Since the death may have occurred quite recently, the chances are good that details of the funeral have not been formulated. Therefore, during this initial telephone call, do not become overly concerned about these details. If the family has already discussed them, they will usually offer readily any information to verify that the details do not present a conflict for the minister or ministers involved. When making contact with the family, you should give them the opportunity to request that you lead the funeral. There will occasionally be some peculiar circumstances when the family might want someone else to do the funeral or, at least, take the leading role. A family member may be a minister, and the family might request this person's leadership, with no insult intended toward anyone else.

Unfortunately, there are occasions when the relationship between a minister and a particular family may be strained and they would simply prefer someone else. On most occasions, fortunately, families want their local minister to lead them during these difficult moments.

If you are separated by great distance or some other extenuating circumstance when you make the initial telephone call, it may be quite appropriate to discuss funeral date and time. However, if you will be with the family in a very short while, the personal visit in their home provides a much better environment to discuss details.

Do not overlook the opportunity to use this initial telephone call as an occasion to pronounce a blessing. Your voice and presence symbolize the warmth of a loving God. Words of assurance carry special significance during these painful moments. With few exceptions most grieving persons want to hear words of assurance from their pastor. In fact, they expect it; so do not hesitate to claim that role. Assure them of your personal concern and the promise of your own prayers.

If you have now established a time to meet with the family, take that time seriously, and be prompt. For most bereaved families, time is precious. There is more to be done than could ever be imagined outside that experience. There will be enough delays and frustrations without their minister being the source of one. Just as you expect them to take your time and schedule seriously, you will want to respect theirs as well.

To be late in getting to the family does more than just create delays. It carries with it the implication that you are insensitive or unconcerned even though you, in actuality, may care tremendously. Promptness is an assumed trademark of any professional. Do not be envisioned as anything less.

The Pastoral Visit

As stated earlier, make this visit as soon as reasonably possible. A prompt visit allows more opportunity for you to be a part of the funeral-service planning process. It is unfortunate when a minister waits hours and, sometimes, days, to make this initial pastoral visit and then becomes frustrated when the details conflict with his own schedule.

There is an even more important reason why this visit should be prompt. Your presence is welcomed and openly received in this setting. Particularly when a relationship has already been established, the family wants you to be with them; they value highly your physical and symbolic presence. You are more than just a friend. You are a tangible reminder of God's love and presence with them. Claim the role which is freely made available to you. The experience can become a very special one.

As you make your way into the presence of the family, do not be timid or shy. Your own strength will find its way into the lives of others. Feelings are passed on like a virus. If you are confident and secure, the family will "catch" some of your strength.

However, there is another principle that needs to be practiced at this point. The strength of a pastor should be a quiet strength! Be careful not to enter the family's presence with a predetermined speech of easy and glib answers. Your entrance is very crucial and should be handled carefully. Your entrance is no less a part of your professional tools than is a scalpel for a surgeon.

Do not enter with a roar. In fact, it is a good

practice once you have acknowledged the presence of people to just sit and develop some sensitivity to the mood of the group. Because of circumstances families will respond to death in a variety of ways. You cannot minister to them unless you make some assessment of their emotional tone and immediate needs. You cannot do this if you enter the room with a need to provide all the answers before the questions have been asked. You are not a drill sergeant or an entertainer. You are the symbolic presence of a calm and peaceful God of love.

As Thomas W. Klink has indicated in his book: *Depth Perspectives in Pastoral Work*, the role of the pastor is one of delicate communication. It is a combination of words, gestures, and actions with which one struggles to convey the fullness of God's word in everyday syllables.[3] An embrace or gentle holding of a grieving person's hand carries more significance than many words. Do not be afraid to just sit and be still with the family. As you begin to converse, there is no harm in inquiring about the circumstances of the death. While the family may not want to relive them with everyone who calls, they will want *you* to know. Do not feel inhibited to ask questions, but allow the bereaved family to share only that with which they are comfortable.

Quite possibly, some of this information will guide the formulating of your words in the funeral service.

Be careful not to offer quick, capsule answers for everything. There are many phrases that have been around for a long time which one might hesitate to quote.

For example, one may speak out of honest concern that "He is better off now because he is with Jesus." Yet the author remembers one lady, who had just lost her husband to cancer, admitting that it made her very angry when someone made that statement to her. "Who are they," she said, "to determine that someone is better off dead?"

Our words in this setting can be a medium of strength and comfort, or they can add pain to an already wounded soul. We must be good stewards of the gift of our words. Do not come up with such inane remarks as, "We just have to accept the Lord's will." One may mean well, but communication at this time must pass through a storm of emotion which very well may cloud one's intention. Beware of quick comments such as: "I know just how you feel."

Dr. R. Lofton Hudson has offered some wise admonition for this setting: "Don't try too hard to console or advise. What most people want when they are in a crisis is somebody *there*, and someone with big ears and a small mouth."[4]

In other words, do not try to take on the role of an all-wise sage. A quiet, strong friend is worth his weight in gold during moments of grief.

This setting now provides an excellent opportunity to discuss the specifics of the funeral service. Ask the family their thoughts about music, Scripture, and any special requests.

Within reasonable limits, the service should be directed toward meeting the needs of the family. Their needs should be foremost at this point. Be as flexible as possible to meet their needs. Do not hesitate to offer advice at points of the planning process. Yet give way to their needs when possible. The service is primarily for the family.

There may be an occasion when the family seems trapped by the emotion of the moment and appears to be making plans that are somewhat inappropriate and could cause some embarrassment in retrospect. Gently question the family concerning the specific detail. If they do not hear your concern, do not press the issue at the moment. This is no time for a tense scene. Instead, let the matter drop momentarily. There is another approach that is usually quite effective.

After leaving the family, contact the funeral director and express your concern to him. He has an accepted entree with the family and can usually influence them in the planning process. Consider the funeral director a partner. Let him help when there is a need. In most circumstances he will offer very gentle guidance to the family. More will be said in another section concerning your relationship to the funeral director.

Visit with the family long enough to effectively communicate your concern and also plan the funeral service. Stay with them long enough to accomplish what needs to be done, but do not "camp out" with the family. Within an appropriate period of time excuse yourself and allow the family to give themselves to the guests who are entering their home.

Before leaving, inquire if there are any other functions you can perform for the family. Are there any persons still needing to be contacted? Is special care needed by a family member who is having difficulty with the news of the death? Should the local church be providing food or hosting the guests?

Make your exit as important as your entrance. A prayer with the family is usually well received and underscores the special role of the minister in that setting. A word of reassurance and a promise of your prayers in the hours ahead will be valued by the family.

Leading the Funeral Service

The minister has a great influence on the quality of the funeral service. The contribution is far more than just a verbal eulogy. The minister's guidance from the planning process to the graveside is sometimes subtle but extremely important.

One should keep in mind that the purpose of a funeral service is to provide support and strength for the bereaved. Certainly, the minister should seek to conduct himself and the service in such a way as to promote an atmosphere of peace and tranquillity. It is not a captive audience to which one must preach one's best evangelistic sermon. It is most unfortunate when ministers use the setting as an opportunity to take a few "shots" at people who might not otherwise frequent the church.

Instead, the funeral service is an ideal setting to convey the love of sympathetic friends and, especially, the love of an incarnate God. The service can become a moment of positive impressions for persons not affiliated with the church.

When a minister takes advantage of the emotions of the moment, everyone loses. Words and gestures should promote the self-sacrificing love of Christ and the symbolic embrace of the believing community.

The service, particularly when conducted in the church, should be characterized as worship. Just as worship takes many forms, so may a funeral service. But it should first and foremost be worship as it points beyond the grief of the moment to a God who is still very much in control of this world. The service should be one of simplicity and brevity. Orderliness should also characterize the service. Thirty to forty-five minutes is ample time for most services. The service should be planned and thought out just as any worship service.

Scripture, appropriately selected, provides comfort to a grieving heart and should be central in any service. Time must be spent in the proper selection as the possibilities for application are many. The analgesic power of Holy Scripture takes on an almost mysterious quality.

Many services will incorporate music. This may include hymns, solos, or special arrangements by organ or piano. Music can be a very meaningful part of a funeral service, but it should be carefully planned. Hymns may be sung by the congregation and should be chosen with discretion.

Do not overlook the possibility of including the eulogy as a separate part within the service. When tastefully done, the eulogy is a very appropriate way of celebrating the deceased person's life. The eulogy is frequently offered separately from and before the sermon and has a valid, traditional role in many services. (More is said about the eulogy later in this chapter.)

The sermon (address) should be well planned by the minister. Too many funeral sermons are quickly thrown together, and the minister misses great opportunities to proclaim the good news of Christ's love. The length of the "sermon" is quite crucial. There is seldom a need for a long address as emotions are usually quite tense. Brevity is a virtue in this setting. Scripture should always form the background for the minister's words. Some possible selections of Scripture are provided in another section of this book. The sharing of a prayer is always appropriate and meaningful. It should not be embellished, and the length should always be given consideration. It is much more than just a good way to signal the funeral director that the service is about to be concluded.

At the conclusion of the service, the minister should lead the recessional from within the church or chapel to the hearse. Once the casket has been placed in the hearse, the minister takes his place in the automobile procession to the graveside. At the graveside, it is customary for the minister to lead the pall-bearers as they carry the casket. The grave-side service, which follows the funeral service, should always be brief. Frequently, friends are standing during the service, which can be a problem if there are extremes of heat or cold with regard to weather. Brief remarks, Scripture, prayer, and a closing committal statement are adequate for the setting. Ten minutes is usually ample time for the grave-side service.

There will be occasions when the entire service will be conducted at the graveside. This type of service, too, requires planning since there are number of circumstances that will be considerably different. For example, the weather, temperature, and seating ar-rangements must always be considered. Usu-ally, most of the people will be standing which necessitates an abbreviated service in comparison with one in the sanctuary.

For such reasons as time, simplicity, and cost there is a significant trend toward a sin-gle service at graveside. Yet even a graveside service deserves the best planning. A well-planned graveside service can be very effec-tive.

The remarks should be delivered from the head end of the casket. After the benediction, the minister usually offers a quiet word of consolation to individual family members seated. A word of blessing or promise of prayer is usually adequate. Several suggested orders of service for the graveside are provided in another section of this book.

The Need for Follow-Up

The opportunities for ministry are not completed once the funeral service and burial have been concluded. In fact, when the formalities have been completed, there is an opportunity for a very special form of ministry. Just as God's care for a bereaved family does not end with the benediction at the funeral service, neither should the compassion of the minister.

Sensitive follow-up will underscore the sincerity of the minister and will create the climate for the development of even stronger relationships with the family. Disappointment may be in store for a grief-stricken family who does not experience the interest of a minister once the formal obligations have been met. It is possible that during the final days of an illness, visits to a particular home were made by the minister with great frequency. When the death occurs, it becomes very easy to forget about a spouse who still has great needs. The minister has possibly already directed his attention to other families where an illness is critical while the spouse of a recently deceased church member is at home wondering why the minister never calls anymore.

With schedules that are already heavy, the minister does not have unlimited time to offer. Yet there are a few simple suggestions that do not require great amounts of time but can communicate a message of love and concern.

After the service has been concluded, make contact with the bereaved and indicate that you will be in touch with them during the next few days. This brief encounter becomes a reminder that they can look forward to your friendship in the tough days ahead.

Keep in mind that this is a very critical time for most persons who have lost a loved one. Immediately following the death, and for the next few days, there is usually a flow of people through the home. There is considerable activity, and it is at this point that the support network seems strongest.

Yet within a short while the house becomes empty. Extended family members return to their homes. Friends must return to their own responsibilities. The house that provided a great deal of defense for the grief process suddenly becomes quiet and very lonely. This is inevitable! The timing then becomes excellent for a pastoral call.

The bereaved one has had some time to think and ask questions of herself and God. It really can become one of those sacred moments when the shepherd and a wounded heart can transact business available to persons only in those two roles. Do not overlook the opportunity for ministry when the house of a grieving family becomes quiet and still. Even a simple telephone call has great value.

Some ministers have disciplined themselves to maintain records that will remind them of the anniversary of a parishioner's death. By recording the date on a calendar they can visit, telephone, or write a letter to the spouse on the anniversary. In most cases the contact will be unexpected and deeply appreciated. The anniversary of a family member's death can be a very difficult experience. Memories are still very strong, and in some cases the grief process is continuing to proceed. A person's knowing that someone else is aware of the pain and offering prayerful support can produce an uplifting experience for a grieving heart. A little extra effort and sensitivity at this point from a minister can become pastoral care at its best.

Relating to the Funeral Director

A good funeral director should be seen by the minister as a partner. He can be a genuine source of help to the family by relieving them of many burdens. There are numerous tasks that the funeral director can perform for the family that otherwise they would have to do themselves. With very few exceptions, funeral directors are very capable and also very caring. They want to assist the family during this time. As a rule, they are very courteous and helpful to the minister as well.

The funeral director will take responsibility for the body and assist the responsible person in making a number of decisions regarding casket, vault, and arrangements. An ethical director will not oversell, particularly at a time when emotions are very strong.

The director will contact relatives, if requested, and will assist in such matters as viewing the body, arranging pallbearers, and notifying the newspaper. He will work out any traffic problems relating to the processional and parking during the funeral service.

It is a good practice for the minister to check signals with the funeral director before every funeral service to verify that all the necessary responsibilities have been fulfilled.

The funeral director, as does the pastor, has a distinct and honorable role to perform.

Occasionally, the question of fees will come up concerning the minister. Most ministers do not even consider the establishing of fees. Instead, they envision grief work as a part of the total ministry whether loved ones of the deceased are church members or not.

Working with Other Ministers

Occasionally, more than one minister will be involved in the funeral setting and, more specifically, the funeral service. A minister should not be threatened or offended by the sharing of duties. Keep in mind that needs of the grieving family must be foremost, and there are many reasons why more than one minister might be asked to participate.

Because ministers tend to relocate on a rather regular basis, a new minister might not have had the opportunity to develop the relationship with the deceased or the family which the previous minister had. The family appreciates and needs the presence of the new minister, yet they may have a strong desire for the support of the previous person whom they have known for a long time.

Our mobile society affects more than the clergy. The deceased may have been a newcomer to the community. It is possible that their membership in the church is quite recent. Therefore, the family might request the assistance of their former, out-of-town minister as well as their new friend.

Occasionally, a minister within the grieving family may be requested to assist and possibly take the lead role. Being a family member will often add warmth and perspective to the funeral service.

Within reasonable limits a minister should try to honor the desires of the family. The time of grief is a critical period with great needs existing for the family. A family will often grasp for the support of as many people as possible. The minister may need to offer some gentle guidance if it appears that the inclusion of people is getting out of hand.

Most families are very open to suggestions by the local minister, and he may need to offer advice to the family. If the minister senses that the number of persons involved in a service is too large, he might want to talk to the funeral director who is usually in a good position to offer suggestions to the family.

The participating ministers should have at least brief conversations before the service to discuss the order of service and expectations of each participant. There is no established protocol as to who initiates the contact. However, the host minister is usually in the best position to make contact with any other persons involved, even including musicians.

Nevertheless, a minister should not view the sharing of responsibilities as a personal threat. With the needs of a family foremost in your mind, you can use the experience as an opportunity to establish new relationships with colleagues. Friendships may be developed as you work together to meet the needs of a grieving family.

Do not envision this circumstance as a sharing of the spotlight. Instead, let it be a team approach to the heavy responsibilities of the moment.

The Value of the Funeral Service

The funeral service, while frequently taken for granted, is a tradition of great value. Even though the form and agenda will vary, there are many reasons why the funeral must be preserved as a part of our culture. It is far more than just an occasion when something nice is said about the deceased.

The Acceptance of Reality

One of the major goals of the funeral service is the facilitating of "grief work." The first segment of the grief journey is that of acceptance, facing up to the reality of death. This fact of human experience must be acknowledged because there is a tendency to deny the reality of death. Denial is our first line of defense when we are faced with the painful reality of death.

One of the values of viewing the body is to confirm the fact that a death has occurred. There are some cultures which actually encourage a family member to kiss the corpse. What appears at first to be a very strange custom may be a tangible way of confirming a death has indeed occurred.

There are stages through which most persons pass as they walk through the "valley of the shadow" of a loved one's death. While it is totally inappropriate to place a timetable on someone, there are observable stages which characterize a healthy journey of grief. The stages of shock, numbness, flood of grief, acceptance, and the return to a new routine provide a sense of direction for the support of a bereaved person.

Repressed grief is very risky. The funeral service should facilitate the grief process. That grief process begins with acceptance, and the funeral service provides a structured, supportive setting for those early hours of grief work.

Viewing the Body

There is also value in the tradition of viewing the body before the funeral service. I encourage family and friends to participate in this tradition for the reason that it puts people in contact with symbols of death. There is a tendency within our culture to insulate the bereaved at the expense of emotional health.

The viewing process is more than just putting a corpse on display. It provides another tangible way of reinforcing the fact that a death has taken place. The practice of viewing the body should not be discouraged in our funeral tradition. The viewing process is usually done at specified times previous to the funeral service. The funeral tradition and wishes of the family will influence the viewing times, especially in regard to the funeral service. In some cases the casket will be open immediately before the service in the chapel or sanctuary. However, the casket should be closed during the funeral service.

As an Expression of Grief

The funeral does much more than work against the denial of death. It also provides an opportunity for family and friends to express their grief. In the process of this expression, there is also opportunity for this same group to offer support and embrace one another.

Within reason there is nothing unseemly about displaying emotions. Naturally, when we have loved someone and lost that person, we are hurt and sad. Pain is a reality of life. Our emotions are a powerful part of our human makeup, and to deny the normal emotionality of human existence is unfair. It is not a sign of weakness to cry. In fact, it may be an indication of care.

Jesus said, "Blessed are those who mourn" (Matt. 5:4). To lament is not necessarily a form of doubting. Holy Scripture is filled with the words of grieving hearts. Listen to the psalmist:

> Hear my prayer, O Lord, and let my cry come unto thee. Hide not they face from me in the day when I am in trouble; incline thine ear unto me: in the day when I call answer me speedily. For my days are consumed like smoke, and my bones are burned as an hearth. My heart is smitten, and withered like grass; so that I forget to eat my bread. By reason of the voice of my groaning my bones cleave to my skin (Ps. 102:1-5, KJV).

On the other hand, do not forget that the psalmist concluded by saying, "But You are the same,/And Your years will have no end./

The children of Your servants will continue,/ And their descendants will be/established before You" (Ps. 102:27-28).

A Christian funeral service provides a ritualized structure by which one can express deep, human sorrow. Jesus reminded us all that those who mourn "shall be comforted" (Matt. 5:4).

Symbolic Embrace of Community

Another positive value of the funeral is the ritual of community support. Most of us take for granted our presence at a funeral. One lady who had just lost her mother stated, "I did not realize how meaningful the presence of my friends at the funeral could be until I was the one seated with the grieving family. I have made a promise to myself to do better by being there for my friends."

Even as friends are seated around the grieving family, their supportive presence becomes a symbolic embrace. The funeral service provides an obvious setting for a supportive network in one of life's toughest moments.

The Funeral as Worship

Above all else the funeral service should be characterized as worship. All of the other positive values would still be inadequate for our needs if the funeral could not take on the act of worship.

The worship of God is the act of giving God His place. He is the Giver of life, the One from whom we came, and the One to whom we go. The time is most appropriate to praise God and offer thanksgiving for sharing the life of a certain individual.

The funeral is a time to be still and know that God is God (see Ps. 46). The setting is a time to listen to what God has to say about life's mysteries and hurts. Through God's Word we can be reassured that the world is not out of control, and that the pain of the moment has not separated us from God or His love.

The funeral becomes worship when the minister holds before the grieving family the priceless gem of Christian hope. The funeral is a setting where much takes place. The acceptance of death, the expression of grief, and the embrace of community are helpful. The priceless nature of the setting comes when Christ is lifted above the pain of the moment. After all, He is the Author and Finisher of our faith. He is the strength for our race, and the goal to which we run. *"O Death, where is your sting? O Hades, where is your victory? . . .* But thanks be to God, who gives us the victory through our Lord Jesus Christ" (1 Cor. 15:55,57).

Collective Grief in the Funeral Setting

A minister should always be aware that in the funeral setting one is dealing with far more than just the immediate and obvious grief. More is involved than just the death of a particular person within the last few days.

The emotion of a funeral service does not take place in a vacuum. As one deals with the present loss, the feelings of all past grief and losses may very well be activated. The grief of the present moment often releases unshed tears of years past.

Consider a man who is attending the funeral because the deceased is the father of his best friend. There will be emotion because he cares for his friend, and he could have been closely associated with the deceased. Yet as he grieves and offers sincere tears for the present loss, he remembers the pain of his own father's death. He begins to discharge old tears under the pretense of the present grief.

The funeral setting has the potential of being an emotional umbrella under which are gathered the feelings of pain in the present and in the past. Realization of this fact adds new potential for ministry in the grief setting, particularly in the funeral service.

The minister can enter the setting with an awareness of a healing ministry that goes beyond the grieving family seated in front of the chapel. Words of hope and comfort are directed to the fresh wounds of the grieving family, but may find their way to scars they assumed had been forgotten.

People weep about present losses. People weep about the losses of childhood. Even more so, people weep about their own mortality. The funeral is the setting where society gives approval to deal with loss in general. To recognize the presence of old tears adds a very precious dimension to ministry.

When the minister enters the pulpit during a funeral service, he addresses a whole room of "losers." Pastoral eyes must be lifted beyond the first few rows all the way to the back of the room. There may be someone on the back row whose pain is old and real. That person has never been willing to give up a loved one to God's care. As the minister speaks, he not only addresses the pain of the identified family but also embraces one who has not forgotten the pain of other years.

The Eulogy

It is unfortunate that a time-honored funeral practice is gradually being abandoned. The eulogy once stood as important as the sermon in traditional funeral services and was granted its own separate place in the service order.

The eulogy was traditionally a celebration of the life of the person now deceased. While the trend now is to include some biographical and factual statements within the sermon, I believe the eulogy should still be granted a place in the service order. There are many reasons why the eulogy has gradually lost its place.

There have been times when the praise of the deceased seemed hollow and "made up." The preacher or friend would strive to catalog the virtues to an extreme, and everyone present knew it. The problem has come with statements which are more laudatory than factual and more fictional than truthful. To avoid the risk of "overdoing," the speaker has chosen the route of keeping it short and saying very little that is personal.

The eulogy, sometimes referred to as the obituary, usually falls within two types. The first tends to be factual: birth, education, career, and honors. The key in preparing this type of eulogy or obituary is the accuracy of facts. Make certain that they come from a dependable source.

The second type of eulogy becomes more of a tribute. This kind of presentation is frequently done by someone other than the minister. More will be said about this possibility later in this section. The tribute focuses upon special attributes that could be observed by the presenting person, or as observed by a particular group for whom one is speaking. The key to success in eulogizing the deceased is understatement. A "swing" that is wider than reality destroys the eulogy's effectiveness. Examples of the two types of eulogies are provided at the end of this section.

The eulogy, when presented tastefully, requires time and effort by the eulogist. The minister does his best eulogy when there was a strong and knowledgeable relationship between himself and the deceased. In many of today's large churches, that kind of relationship with many members is not likely. Yet there are ways of approaching a eulogy even when there is little knowledge of the deceased. This can be accomplished for the minister through prompt and brief interviews with family and friends.

The interviews should not be detached, fact-finding missions with legal pads and tape recorders. The interviews should be simple and straightforward, with the focus on the survivor's memories. The question: "How are you feeling?" is a good way to begin. Allow the person to share feelings about the deceased, especially those related to events surrounding the death. This kind of sharing may become an emotional time. Do not be afraid of these emotions.

These conversations accomplish two functions. They provide information that can be used as a part of the eulogy. There is also the opportunity for therapy as the one interviewed remembers the life of the deceased. Talking about these events often helps to heal the hurts of the moment and facilitates the grief process. Good judgment must be exercised as you select information to share as a part of the eulogy. Some information may need family approval to be shared. One should give special interest to material that deals with the character of the deceased.

By a Friend

Not uncommon is the request for a friend of the deceased to be requested to give the eulogy. This approach frequently adds a very special touch to the funeral service. The friend can talk from a perspective that is open and honest.

If the friend of the deceased has never presented a eulogy before he may have questions as to how it is done. The minister should offer guidance in the matter. A few suggestions might be made. For example, the friend should remember the context from which he speaks. He should not deliver the minister's "sermon." His words should reflect the perspective that comes from being a friend of the deceased. As a friend he has made observations that are unique. The process can become a tender sharing of a life and a relationship. Encouragement should be given toward brevity, clarity, and integrity. Remember that the goal is to celebrate life and the person.

Appropriate Humor

The eulogy need not focus only on the serious aspects of life and death. After all, life is a mixture of the serious and the humorous. Particularly if the deceased was a humorous person, do not be afraid to share some of the pleasant and funny memories. But take care that you do not turn it into a joke session. It is one thing to share tender humor, but another to tell jokes that may be totally inappropriate. One must be sensitive to the emotions and needs of the moment.

Carefully chosen humor not only helps one remember special characteristics of the deceased, but it can help cut through the tension of a funeral setting. I remember conducting a funeral service when the tension was very obvious. The deceased was a sweet lady for whom everyone really cared. She was a very jovial person, and was known by everyone for her hats. She had dozens of hats and always wore one whenever she came to church. During the eulogy the question was raised—Which had she was wearing when she met Saint Peter? The congregation knew the spirit in which the comment was made, and all shared a moment of laughter. After the laughter the tension had been reduced, and the service was more relaxed for everyone.

Humor must be carefully chosen. It must be well placed and never used in any way other than to celebrate the deceased. Ridicule and barbed humor have no place in a funeral service.

In summary, a well-prepared and well-presented eulogy will bring mourners together and bring to mind memories of a life, although now ended, which can be claimed and celebrated.

Example One: Biographical Style

This first type of eulogy or obituary is a summary of the important facts of an individual's life. Included in these facts should be references to the person's birth, education, affiliations, interests, family relationship, professional concerns, and honors. These facts should be gathered from dependable sources and presented by someone thoroughly familiar with the deceased, preferably by the minister.

Example Two: Tribute Style

EULOGY
Mrs. W. H. Walls
June 19, 1986

(Delivered by Her Grandson)

Myron Madden in his book *The Power to Bless* has indicated that grief turns adults back toward childhood.[5] There is a tendency to dream of times long past when the world seemed young and untroubled. A man's childhood is as available in his mind as are present days. There is a strange tranquillity that comes from escaping into early years.

I find myself right now surrounded by the remembrances of early years. This town used to be home. This church used to be the church I attended. One summer during college I even worked with the crew that built the wing behind us. There are names of people and familiar faces that are so very natural and make one feel that some things really do transcend time.

There is no way to mentally return to those days without some persons being firmly in the middle of those memories. For me and for some of you the Lady we come today to remember is one of those persons. There is no way for me to escape back in memory without her being there. Of all roles that any person plays, her role as grandmother is such a powerful role for me that I have difficulty in seeing her as anything except Grandmother.

Grandmothers are special people. I am one of the fortunate ones because I was given two beautiful ones. Their influence upon my life is not subtle but profound. And I count it as a gift of God, to whom I will forever be grateful.

I cannot come to this setting today without being aware of my indebtedness. I am indebted to her for being what grandmothers are supposed to be: kind, gentle, trusting, and making few demands in return. I, along with many of you, have experienced all these from Cora Walls.

Her home always seemed like home. It looked, smelled, and just felt like a home should be. In some ways it appeared to be unchanged by time. And yet deep down we all know that nothing material or mortal evades the hands of the clock. We only fool and deceive ourselves to think otherwise.

One of the most difficult challenges of growing is the acceptance of the fact that life changes. It is the first challenge we face out of our mother's womb and the last one we face before entering the outstretched arms of our Lord. We don't always like change, and, to be honest, I don't think God expects us to do so. We only have to accept it and move on. There is always the overarching challenge to move on.

Such is our great challenge today. And of all the ways that we could honor this Lady, nothing would dignify her passing more than taking what she has given and move on. She has given so much. In the past few hours as I have tried to recall all that has come to me through her, I kept coming back to the fact that she has simply given herself. To try to break it down into the many things that she has done and been for so many of us seems to discredit her most valuable gift: herself. And she never hesitated to make that offer.

For me as with you I must now take all that she has invested in me, gently wrap it up, and let it become one of life's treasures, and keep it within me where neither "rust doth corrupt, [nor] thieves break through and steal."

Since it became obvious that her death was

impending, I have asked myself what kind of
response is appropriate for my grandmother.
Such a special person deserves a distinct response. I can only speak for myself, but I have
chosen to honor her by giving her up. As long
as a person holds to his loved one who has
died, he holds himself against all spiritual
blessings.

The essence of despair is in putting God in
the past tense. We do ourselves, our faith, and
our deceased loved ones an injustice when we
let the past override the future. Just as God
has cared for Cora Walls all through her life,
He will now care for her in death.

I believe that very strongly. Just as He has
cared for you He will continue to embrace
you with His mercies. The curse of grief can
only be removed when we become con-
vinced and rest on the assurance that even
the power of death is not too great for God's
blessings to prevail.

This is how I have chosen to respond to this
event in my life and your lives. I will give her
up and give her back to a Lord who has been
her personal Friend for eighty-eight years.
We must take her gifts with us and not only
embrace them, but incorporate them.

I will leave here today very much aware
that our lives are not islands unto themselves,
that we bear the influence of special people in

our lives. We will honor her best by leaving this place and going back to work. But we leave realizing that to this date we have been blessed by the presence of a gentle spirit.

Notes

1. Used by permission from Dr. John R. Claypool.
2. Dr. Wayne Oates, *The Christian Pastor* (Philadelphia: Westminster Press, 1964), p. 47.
3. Thomas W. Klink, *Depth Perspectives in Pastoral Work* (Englewood Cliffs, N.J.: Prentice-Hall, 1965), p. 17.
4. Lofton Hudson, *Persons in Crisis.* (Nashville: Broadman Press, 1969), p. 17.
5. Myron C. Madden, *The Power to Bless* (Nashville: Broadman Press, 1970), p. 104.

2
Suggested Orders
of Service

The funeral setting is, first and foremost, a service of worship. The funeral service is not one single dynamic but many. Yet the primary function of the service should be to lift the eyes of those who mourn beyond the pain of the moment to a God who is victorious in life and death. A well-planned service which celebrates life in Christ now and life in Christ to come will be extremely valuable moments.

In the Sanctuary or Chapel

I.

Piano or Organ Music
Opening Scriptural Sentences
Invocation
Special Music
Scripture Readings
Eulogy
Prayer
Message
Benediction

II.

Piano or Organ Music
Vocal Selection
Scripture Readings
Prayer
Vocal Selection
Message
Closing Prayer

III.

Piano or Organ Music
Opening Scriptural Sentences
Congregational Hymn
Scripture Readings
Eulogy
Prayer
Message
Vocal Selection
Benediction

IV.

Piano or Organ Music
Vocal Selection
Recitation of the Lord's Prayer
Eulogy
Scripture Readings
Pastoral Prayer
Vocal Selection
Message

Benediction

V. (for two ministers)

Piano or Organ Music
Scripture and Remarks by First Minister
Prayer
Vocal Selection
Message by Second Minister
Benediction

VI.

Piano or Organ Music
Opening Scriptural Sentences
Invocation
Hymn
Eulogy Delivered by a Friend
Pastoral Prayer
Special Music
Message
Benedicition

VII. (no special music)

Piano or Organ Music
Invocation
Recitation of the Lord's Prayer
Old And New Testament Readings
Message
Benediction

At Graveside

At the graveside the minister will usually take his place at the hearse and precede the casket to the grave. Then he will take his place at the head of the grave and face the family to deliver his remarks.

Following the benedicition, the minister will customarily speak quietly to the seated immediate family members before the funeral director indicates the other guests may come forward to visit with the family. As the minister speaks briefly to the individual family members, a simple word of assurance or blessing is appropriate.

I.

Opening Scriptural Sentences
Invocation
Old and New Testament Readings
Apostle's Creed
Eulogy
Committal
Benediction

II.

Scripture
Committal
Prayer
Scriptural Benediction

Service Only at Graveside

When following a service in the church or funeral chapel, the graveside service should be very brief. Under such circumstances the graveside service becomes the conclusion of the previous service with the emphasis on the committal of the body.

If the graveside setting is the entire service and there was no previous gathering at the church or chapel, the minister may take longer for the service. Even under these circumstances, brevity must be considered since some guests are likely to be standing. Once again, common sense should guide one's leadership in these moments.

At the graveside the minister might make use of the natural setting to call attention to God's care and involvement in our world. Regardless of the season, signs of life are always very obvious and symbolic of God's power, even in times that appear to signify the end of life.

I. Committal at Graveside

Forasmuch as it has pleased Almighty God to take unto himself the soul of our friend, we offer the body to this place prepared for it, that ashes may return to ashes, dust to dust, and the imperishable spirit may forever be with the Lord.

II. Committal at Graveside

We gather here to claim memories which are forever sacred as they are a gift of God. We are supported by a faith stronger than death, sustained by the hope of a life that extends eternally beyond this place. Within that confidence, we gather here to commit all that is mortal of our friend to this resting place, surrounded by the handiwork of God in nature, yet aware that we have a resting place not made with hands but by God Eternal.

III. Committal at Graveside

It is not by choice that we gather in this city of the dead, hallowed by the sacred memory of its inhabitants. The monuments are only symbols of the affection of surviving friends. The absence of the souls of these inhabitants is but a monument to a loving and life-giving God. As we offer the body of our deceased we are reminded that there is life immortal that shall indeed survive the grave. We now commit this one to the arms of a God who gives life that never ends.

3
Suggested Scripture Readings

Opening Scriptural Sentences

The eternal God is your refuge,
And underneath are
   the everlasting arms;
He will thrust out the enemy
   from before you (Deut. 33:27).

"Have I not commanded you? Be strong and of good courage; do not be afraid, nor be dismayed, for the Lord your God is with you wherever you go" (Josh. 1:9).

And he said:
"Naked I came from my mother's
   womb,
And naked shall I return there.
The Lord gave, and the Lord
   has taken away;
Blessed be the name of the Lord" (Job 1:21).

Who may ascend into the hill of the
   Lord?
Or who may stand in His holy place?

He who has clean hands and a pure
  heart,
Who has not lifted up his soul to an
  idol,
Nor sworn deceitfully.
He shall receive blessing from the
  Lord,
And righteousness from the God of his
  salvation (Ps. 24:3-5).

The Lord is my light and my
  salvation;
Whom shall I fear?
The Lord is the strength of my life;
Of whom shall I be afraid (Ps. 27:1)?

I will lift up my eyes to the hills—
From whence comes my help?
My help comes from the Lord,
Who made heaven and earth (Ps. 121:1-2).

The Lord is near to all who call upon
  Him,
To all who call upon Him in truth (Ps.
145:18).

Fear not, for I am with you;
Be not dismayed, for I am your God.
I will strengthen you,
Yes, I will help you,
I will uphold you with My righteous
  right hand (Isa. 41:10).

Jesus said to her, "I am the resurrection

and the life. He who believes in Me, though he may die, he shall live" (John 11:25).

"Let not your heart be troubled; you believe in God, believe also in Me" (John 14:1).

For we know that if your earthly house, this tent, is destroyed, we have a building from God, a house not made with hands, eternal in the heavens (2 Cor. 5:1).

But has now been revealed by the appearing of our Savior Jesus Christ, who has abolished death and brought life and immortality to light through the gospel (2 Tim. 1:10).

Selected Readings

The Lord is my shepherd;
I shall not want.
He makes me to lie down in green
      pastures;
He leads me beside the still waters.
He restores my soul;
He leads me in the paths of
      righteousness
For His name's sake.

Yea, though I walk through the valley
      of the shadow of death,
I will fear no evil;
For You are with me;
Your rod and Your staff,
      they comfort me.
You prepare a table before me in the

presence of my enemies;
You anoint my head with oil;
My cup runs over.
Surely goodness and mercy shall
follow me
All the days of my life;
And I will dwell in the house
of the Lord
Forever (Ps. 23).

God is our refuge and strength,
A very present help in trouble.
Therefore we will not fear,
Though the earth be removed,
And though the mountains be carried
into the midst of the sea;
Though its waters roar and be troubled,
Though the mountains shake with its
swelling.   Selah

There is a river whose streams shall
make glad the city of God,
The holy place of the tabernacle of the
Most High.
God is in the midst of her,
she shall not be moved;
God shall help her,
just at the break of dawn.
The nations raged, the kingdoms were
moved;
He uttered His voice, the earth melted.

The Lord of Hosts is with us;
The God of Jacob is our refuge.   Selah

Come, behold the works of the Lord,
Who has made desolations in the earth.
He makes wars cease to the end of the
   earth;
He breaks the bow
   and cuts the spear in two;
He burns the chariot in the fire.

Be still, and know that I am God;
I will be exalted among the nations,
I will be exalted in the earth!

The Lord of hosts is with us;
The God of Jacob is our refuge.   Selah
   (Ps. 46)

   Lord, You have been our dwelling place
      in all generations.
   Before the mountains were brought
      forth,
   Or ever You had formed the earth and
      the world,
   Even from everlasting to everlasting
      You are God (Ps. 90:1-2).

   The days of our lives are seventy years;
   And if by reason of strength they are
      eighty years,
   Yet their boast is only labor and
      sorrow;
   For soon it is cut off, and we fly away (Ps.
   90:10).

      How can a young man cleanse his
         way?

By taking heed according to Your
word.
With my whole heart I have sought
You;
Oh, let me not wander from Your
commandments!
Your word I have hidden in my heart,
That I might not sin against You.
Blessed are You, O Lord!
Teach me Your statutes (Ps. 119:9-12).

I will lift up my eyes to the hills—
From whence comes my help?
My help comes from the Lord,
Who made heaven and earth.

He will not allow your foot to be
moved;
He who keeps you will not slumber.
Behold, He who keeps Israel
Shall neither slumber nor sleep.

The Lord is your keeper;
The Lord is your shade at your right
hand.
The sun shall not strike you by day,
Nor the moon by night.

The Lord shall preserve you from all
evil;
He shall preserve your soul.
The Lord shall preserve your going
out and your coming in
From this time forth,

and even forevermore (Ps. 121).

The Lord upholds all who fall,
And raises up all those who are bowed
　　down.
The eyes of all look expectantly to
　　You,
And You give them their food in due
　　season.
You open Your hand
And satisfy the desire of every living
　　thing.

....

The Lord is near to all who call upon
　　Him,
To all who call upon Him in truth (Ps.
145:14-16,18).

Who can find a virtuous wife?
For her worth is far above rubies.
The heart of her husband safely trusts
　　her;
So he will have no lack of gain.
She does him good and not evil
All the days of her life.

....

Her children rise up
　　and call her blessed;
Her husband also, and he praises her:
"Many daughters have done well,
But you excel them all."
Charm is deceitful and beauty is vain,
But a woman who fears the Lord,

she shall be praised.
Give her of the fruit of her hands,
And let her own works praise her in
    the gates (Prov. 31:10-12,28-31).

Have you not known?
Have you not heart?
The everlasting God, the Lord,
The Creator of the ends of the earth,
Neither faints nor is weary.
There is no searching of His
    understanding.
He gives power to the weak,
And to those who have no might
    He increases strength.
Even the youths shall faint
    and be weary,
And the young men shall utterly fall,
But those who wait on the Lord
Shall renew their strength;
They shall mount up with wings like
    eagles,
They shall run and not be weary,
They shall walk and not faint (Isa.
40:28-31).

"The Lord is my portion,"
    says my soul,
"Therefore I hope in Him!"

The Lord is good to those
    who wait for Him,
To the soul who seeks Him.
It is good that one should hope

and wait quietly
For the salvation of the Lord (Lam.
3:24-26).

"Come to Me, all you who labor and are
heavy laden, and I will give you rest. Take
My yoke upon you and learn from Me, for I
am gentle and lowly in heart, and you will
find rest for your souls. For My yoke is easy
and My burden is light (Matt. 11:28-30)."

"But of that day and hour no one knows,
neither the angels in heaven, nor the Son,
but only the Father. Take heed, watch and
pray; for you do not know when the time is.
It is like a man going to a far country, who
left his house and gave authority to his servants, and to each his work and commanded
the doorkeeper to watch. Watch therefore,
for you do not know when the master of the
house is coming—in the evening, at mid-
night, at the crowing of the rooster, or in the
morning—lest, coming suddenly, he find you
sleeping. And what I say to you, I say to all:
Watch!" (Mark 13:32-37).

"Blessed are those servants whom the
master, when he comes, will find watching.
Assuredly, I say to you that he will gird himself and have them sit down to eat, and will
come and serve them. And if he should come
in the second watch, or come in the third
watch, and find them so, blessed are those

servants. But know this, that if the master of the house had known what hour the thief would come, he would have watched and not allowed his house to be broken into. Therefore you also be ready, for the Son of Man is coming at an hour you do not expect. . . . Blessed is that servant whom his master will find so doing when he comes. Truly, I say to you that he will make him ruler over all that he has" (Luke 12:37-40,43-44).

Jesus said to her, "Your brother will rise again." Martha said to Him, "I know that he will rise again in the resurrection at the last day." Jesus said to her, "I am the resurrection and the life. He who believes in Me, though he may die, he shall live" (John 11:23-25).

"Let not your heart be troubled; you believe in God, believe also in Me. In My Father's house are many mansions; if it were not so, I would have told you. I go to prepare a place for you. And if I go and prepare a place for you, I will come again and receive you to Myself; that where I am, there you may be also. And where I go you know, and the way you know." Thomas said to Him, "Lord, we do not know where You are going, and how can we know the way?" Jesus said to him, "I am the way, the truth, and the life. No one comes to the Father except through Me." (John 14:1-6).

Now He who has prepared us for this very thing is God, who also has given us the Spirit as a guarantee. Therefore we are always confident, knowing that while we are at home in the body we are absent from the Lord. For we walk by faith, not by sight. We are confident, yes, well pleased rather to be absent from the body and to be present with the Lord (2 Cor. 5:5-8).

But I do not want you to be ignorant, brethren, concerning those who have fallen asleep, lest you sorrow as others who have no hope. For if we believe that Jesus died and rose again, even so God will bring with Him those who sleep in Jesus. For this we say to you by the word of the Lord, that we who are alive and remain until the coming of the Lord will by no means precede those who are asleep. For the Lord Himself will descend from heaven with a shout, with the voice of an archangel, and with the trumpet of God. And the dead in Christ will rise first. Then we who are alive and remain shall be caught up together with them in the clouds to meet the Lord in the air. And thus we shall always be with the Lord. Therefore comfort one another with these words (1 Thess. 4:13-18).

For I am already being poured out as a drink offering, and the time of my departure is at hand. I have fought the good fight, I have finished the race, I have kept the faith.

Finally, there is laid up for me the crown of righteousness, which the Lord, the righteous Judge, will give to me on that Day, and not to me only but also to all who have loved His appearing (2 Tim. 4:6-8).

Here is the patience of the saints; here are those who keep the commandments of God and the faith of Jesus. Then I heard a voice from heaven saying to me, "Write: 'Blessed are the dead who die in the Lord from now on.'" "Yes," says the Spirit, "that they may rest from their labors, and their works follow them" (Rev. 14:12-13).

And I saw a new heaven and a new earth, for the first heaven and the first earth had passed away. Also there was no more sea. Then I, John, saw the holy city, New Jerusalem, coming down out of heaven from God, prepared as a bride adorned for her husband. And I heard a loud voice from heaven saying, "Behold, the tabernacle of God is with men, and He will dwell with them, and they shall be His people, and God Himself will be with them and be their God. And God will wipe away every tear from their eyes; there shall be no more death, nor sorrow, nor crying; and there shall be no more pain, for the former things have passed away." Then He who sat on the throne said, "Behold, I make all things new." And He said to me, "Write, for these words are true and faithful" (Rev. 21:1-5).

"And behold, I am coming quickly, and My reward is with Me, to give to every one according to his work. I am the Alpha and the Omega, the Beginning and the End, the First and the Last." Blessed are those who do His commandments, that they may have the right to the tree of life, and may enter through the gates into the city (Rev. 22:12-14).

4
A Collection of Appropriate Poems

Lord, be Thou near and cheer my lonely way;
  With Thy sweet peace my aching bosom fill;
Scatter my cares and fears; my grief allay,
    And be it mine each day
    To love and please Thee still.

—P. Corneille

O Lord, how happy is the time
    When in Thy love I rest:
When from my weariness I climb
    E'en to Thy tender breast.
The night of sorrow endeth there,
    Thy rays outshine the sun;
And in Thy pardon and Thy care
    The heaven of heavens is won.

—W. C. Dessler

Those Mansions Above

We strain every nerve, we strive for the prize
Of our calling in Christ: a home in the skies:

The battles all fought, the victory won,
We have the reward—"Good servant, well done:"

"Come, enter thy home, these mansions above,
Rest in the haven of infinite love;
From sorrow and sin forever released,
Come sit with the guests at the heavenly feast."

All stains washed away, in robes of pure white
We bask in His rays, we shine in His light;
The crown of rejoicing we evermore wear,
The glory of Christ eternally share.

Make me, O Father, more grateful for life,
More willing to bear the turmoil and strife,
More anxious to serve, more like Him to be
Who gave His own life a ransom for me.

That, bearing Christ's image, e'en here below,
My word done in Him, His glory may show,
Till the summons I hear, in accents of love,
"Daughter, come higher, and serve Me above."

What glories await the spirit set free
From fetters of earth, untrammelled to be!
The work begun here is continued above,
And all that blest life is service and love.

—Parish Visitor

Be still, my soul!—The Lord is on thy side;
   Bear patiently the cross of grief and
pain;
Leave to thy God to order and provide,—
   In every change He faithful will remain.
      —Hymns from the Land of Luther

God's Sure Help in Sorrow

    Leave all to God,
Forsaken one, and stay thy tears;
   For the Highest knows thy pain,
Sees thy suffering and thy fears;
    Thou shalt not wait His help in vain;
    Leave all to God.

    Be still and trust!
For His strokes are strokes of love,
   Thou must for thy profit bear;
He thy filial fear would move,
    Trust thy Father's loving care,
    Be still and trust!

    Know God is near!
Though thou think'st Him far away,
   Though His mercy long hath slept,
He will come and not delay,
    When His child enough hath wept,
    For God is near!

    Oh, teach Him not
When and how to hear thy prayers;
   Never doth our God forget;

He the cross who longest bears
  Finds his sorrow's bounds are set;
    Then teach Him not!

If thou love Him,
Walking truly in His ways,
  Then no trouble, cross or death
E'er shall silence faith and praise;
  All things serve thee here beneath,
    If thou love God!

—Anon

My Child of Promise

My child, My precious child,
I loved and planned your life from the
very beginning.
Even before I formed the mountains and
created the earth.
I had a purpose for your life on earth.

I love you, that I gave My only begotten
Son for you.
The sacrifice of the cross, He paid for you.
My plan for you is eternal and everlasting.
Each step you take and every detail of
your life, I know.

It may be on the top of the mountain,
where the storms may
  blow.
It may be in the valley where the pleasant
brooks flow.
Remember this, wherever I plant you,
there is a purpose

and a plan that will continue until I return
for you.
So praise Me with love and adoration.

Sing praises unto My name.
Taste of the everlasting water that is yours
and is freely
    given.
Lean upon Me.
Trust and have faith in Me.

Draw unto Me and let My everlasting arms
surround you and
    uplift you.
Know, that I am everlasting, and My love
never changes.
Someday, you shall be planted in My
garden of eternal love.
My child, My precious child
Rejoice!

—Beverly Thieme

Teach me your mood, O patient stars!
    Who climb each night the ancient sky
Leaving on space no shade, no scars,
    No trace of age, no fear to die.
                    —Ralph Waldo Emerson

A Mother's Love

A Mother's love, how sweet the name!
What is a mother's love?
A noble, pure, and tender flame,
Enkindled from above,
To bless a heart of earthly mould;

The warmest love that cannot grow cold;
This is a mother's love.

—James Montgomery

A Mother's Love

Like a cradle rocking, rocking,
Silent, peaceful, to and fro;
Like a mother's sweet looks dropping
On the little face below,
Hangs the green earth, swinging, turning,
Jarless, noiseless, safe and slow;
Falls the light of God's face bending
Down and watching us below.
And as feeble babes that suffer,
Toss and cry, and will not rest,
Are the ones the tender mother
Holds the closest, loves the best:
So, when we are weak and wretched,
By our sins weighed down, distressed,
Then it is that God's great patience
Holds us closest, loves us best.

—Saxe Holm

Content

Think'st thou the man whose mansions
hold
The Worlding's pomp and miser's gold,
Obtains a richer prize
Than he, who, in his cot at rest
Finds heavenly peace a willing guest,
And bears the promise in his breast
Of treasure in the skies?

—L. H. Sigourney

I hold it true, whate'er befall,
I fell it when I sorrow most—
'Tis better to have loved and lost
Than never to have loved at all.
—Alfred Tennyson

Death's but a path that must be trod
If man would ever pass to God.
—Thomas Parness

Our Dear Ones

God gives us ministers of love,
Which we regard not, being near;
Death takes them from us, then we feel
That angels have been with us here!

A babe in a house is a wellspring of
pleasure,
A messenger of peace and love,
A resting-place for innocence on earth; a
link
Between angels and men.
—M. F. Tupper

How to Live

So live, that when thy summons comes to
join
The innumerable caravan that moves
To that mysterious realm, where each shall
take
His chamber in the silent halls of death,

Thou go not like the quarry-slave at night,
Scourged to his dungeon, but, sustained
and soothed
By an unfaltering trust, approach thy
grave,
Like one that wraps the drapery of his
couch
About him, and lies down to pleasant
dreams.

—William C. Bryant

My Father's House

"Let not your heart be troubled," then He
said,
"My Father's house has mansions large and
fair;
I go before you to take you with Me
there."
And since that hour, the awful foe is
charmed,
And life and death are glorified and fair;
Whither He went, we know—the way we
know,
And with firm step press on to meet Him
there.

—Mrs. H. B. Stowe

My knowledge of that life is small,
The eye of faith is dim,
But 'tis enough that Christ knows all,
And I shall be with Him.

—Baxter

Calmly we look behind us, on joys and
sorrows past,
We know that all is mercy now, and shall
be well at last;
Calmly we look before us, —we fear no
future ill,
Enough for safety and for peace, if Thou
art with us still.

—Jane Borthwick

Under Thy wings, my God, I rest,
Under Thy shadow safely lie;
By Thy own strength in peace possessed,
While dreaded evils pass me by.

—A. L. Waring

The Bravest Battle

The bravest battle that ever was fought
Shall I tell you where and when?
On the maps of the world you will find it
not,
It was fought by the mothers of men.
Nay, not with cannon nor battle-shot
With sword, or nobler pen;
Nay not with eloquent words of thought
From mouths of wonderful men.

But deep in a walled-up woman's heart
A woman who would not yield,
But bravely, silently bore her part—
Lo! There was the battlefield!
No marshalling troops, no bivouac song—

No banners to gleam and wave—
But, oh! these battles, they last so long—
  From babyhood to the grave.

Yet faithful still as a bridge of stars
  She fights in her walled-up town.
Fights on and on in her endless wars,
  Then, silent, unseen, goes down.

Oh, Ye, with banners and battle-shot
  With soldiers to shout and praise,
I tell you the kingliest victories wrought
  Are won in these silent ways.

Oh, spotless woman, in a world of shame
  With splendid and silent scorn,
Go back to God as pure as you came
  The queenliest warrior born.

                —Joaquin Miller

In "pastures green"? Not always;
sometimes He
Who knoweth best, in kindness leadeth me
In weary ways, where heavy shadows be.
So, whether on the hilltops high and fair
I swell, or in the sunless valleys, where
The shadows lie, what matter? He is there.

                —Henry H. Barry

Be trustful, be steadfast, whatever betide
thee,
  Only one thing do thou ask of the
Lord,—
Grace to go forward wherever He guide
thee,

Simply believing the truth of His word.
—Anon.

Lead, kindly Light, amid the encircling
gloom,
  Lead Thou me on;
The night is dark, and I am far from home,
  Lead Thou me on:
Keep Thou my feet; I do not ask to see
The distant scene—one step enough for
me.

—John Henry Newman

O Lord, how happy should we be
If we could cast our care on Thee,
  If we from self could rest;
And feel at heart that One above,
In perfect wisdom, perfect love,
  Is working for the best.

—Joseph Antice

Oh, ask not thou, How shall I bear
  The burden of tomorrow?
Sufficient for today, its care,
  Its evil and its sorrow;
God imparteth by the way
Strength sufficient for the day.

—Jane E. Saxby

Speak Lord, for Thy servant heareth,
  Speak peace to my anxious soul,
And help me to feel that all my ways
  Are under Thy wise control;

That He who cares for the lily,
  And heeds the sparrow's fall,
Shall tenderly lead His loving child:
  For He made and loveth all.

—Anon.

To heaven I lift my waiting eyes;
  There all my hopes are laid;
The Lord that built the earth and skies
  Is my perpetual aid.

—Isaac Watts

5
Guiding Thoughts
for the Funeral Setting

A. Walking Through the Valley
Text: Psalm 23
Focus: Psalm 23:4

Most of us are aware that this psalm is read quite frequently in memorial settings. The use of the psalm is no accident, and neither is the frequent use due to habit. The psalmist has provided for us a word of hope that goes beyond the limits of life into the shadows which appear for every human being.

Assuming that David is the author of this masterpiece, one must consider the background he brought to his words. David was a mortal creature with joys and frustrations. He was a powerful person physically and politically. He was a king and a servant of God. He was also a man of confidence because he had allowed life to teach him well the lessons of faith. He not only had confidence in himself, but as a man of great faith he had tremendous confidence in God.

We can only speculate as to the immediate circumstances of this psalm. Whatever the immediate occasion it was one of those times when the very foundations of life seemed to be threatened. Yet the psalmist spoke with such assurance, an assurance for which most of us hunger.

Consider his carefully chosen description of death. Not a word was wasted as he pointed us to the only Source of confidence in those times. He spoke of death in several ways.

He talked of his "walk through the valley of the shadow of death." The fact that he described the place as a valley is significant. Of all the possibilities of places, the psalmist selected the visual image of a valley. He did not describe death in terms of a violent sea, a stormy mountain, nor a lifeless desert. He painted the image of a valley, that area at the foot of a peaceful mountain. It is not far from the mountain where we can more easily envision the omnipotent God of peace.

The psalmist continued the sermon in his description of death as a shadow. The image he offered is such a powerful one. While others of his day spoke of the chambers of death or the gates of death, David became a pioneer as he defined the tense power of death by relegating it to only a shadow.

Do keep in mind that a shadow exists only as long as there is light to cast a shadow. The Lord was not only David's Shepherd who supplied his wants but also the only Source of light. Regardless of its nature, death only temporarily stands in our light. The light is still there. A shadow is evidence of its existence. What a reassuring image of this force we seem to fear!

Yet, one of the most significant words in Psalm 23 is one that we frequently read past without giving much thought to the reassurance which is offered. The psalmist spoke of a walk through the valley. It is not a walk *into* the valley. It is not a walk *in* the valley. It is not even a walk *around* the valley. Instead, the journey is *through* the valley. This image has to be one of the most powerful in all of Scripture.

The journey is temporary. The writer did not go into detail concerning time. The length of the walk becomes insignificant once the discovery is made that the journey is only temporary. We can persevere as long as we can see light at the end of the tunnel. That light is always there.

The walk you are experiencing today is a temporary one. The valley of the shadow is all about you. But you must keep in mind that this segment is not an endless journey. You, too, will soon walk into the light which has only been momentarily blocked.

The basis for our hope is found in the fact that the Shepherd is walking with us. We are not alone in these circumstances or in any other. The Shepherd has not only walked before us but preparations have been made for our necessities, even now as we meet here. There is little in life more frightening than loneliness. Our walk is not a solo. There is the best of company for our journey. A caring Shepherd will comfort us with his rod and staff.

There is little in life that isolates us more than the pain of grief. Yet this psalm is a vivid reminder that His rod and staff are providing for our needs this very moment. A loved one for whom there is genuine grief will not return on this side of the door. But, in the meantime as you adjust to that absence, the Shepherd will be caring for you and your loved one every moment.

There is no mystery as to why this great psalm is embraced so frequently in this setting. In this moment there are great needs for green pastures and still waters. The psalmist pointed us to a Shepherd who does more than just tend to us. He laid down His life for us.

The path we walk today is not an uncharted way. Preparations began long ago as He seeks even now to restore our souls.

So it is with our loved one in whose memory we gather. Remember, the Good Shepherd has not only carried this one into, but *through* the shadow.

Prayer: Lord, help us to see death as it really is—only a shadow. Most of all, help us to trust the Shepherd who has experienced and understands all mysteries—in whose name we offer our prayer. Amen.

B. Living and Dying in Christ
Text: Philippians 1:19-26
Focus: Philippians 1:21

Entirely too often the family of God gathers in this memorial setting. This kind of gathering is never easy, for it is a time of mixed emotions. Certainly there is no pleasure in gathering to bid good-bye to someone who is very special. This moment is a time of loss. An investment has been made into the life of someone, and now that someone has been called home to our Lord.

Yet grief is not the only agenda today. This setting takes on an entirely different meaning for a Christian because we gather in the midst of hope, the hope that comes from our faith in the life, death, and resurrection of our Lord Jesus Christ.

This time is also one when we let God's Word speak to us. We turn to His Word, not because there is a lack of anything else to read. Rather, we need the Bible because it is a Book about life and death. Just as the Bible is very frank and honest about life, so is it also very honest about death. The Bible never tiptoes around the issue of death. Consider the psalmist as he spoke so very freely about our walking in and through the valley of the shadow of death. This walk was not to be seen as something awesome, but rather simply a part of the journey which everyone must make.

Other than Christ, no one ever spoke more frankly about death than the apostle Paul. He understood all of life to be in the control of Christ, and, therefore, death was just as natural process by which we leave one state and enter into another.

Paul made one statement about death that is as bold as any we shall ever read. He said,

"For to me, to live is Christ, and to die is gain" (Phil. 1:21). The assumption is that Paul was in prison awaiting trial when he made this statement, and he had to face the fact that he was quite uncertain whether he would live or die. However, to him the matter made little difference. His indifference was not the result of some sick attitude about life. Paul enjoyed living as much as anyone. However, he saw living and dying all within the loving arms of God.

For Paul, living gained meaning through Christ. For him, living was Christ, and life could not be separated from his Lord. For Paul, Christ had been the beginning of his life. He was born again on the Damascus road. Life had literally begun all over for him. From that moment on, Christ had become the sustaining element of his life. There had never been a day since that experience when Paul had not lived under His presence. For Paul, Christ had also become the reason for his existence. Christ was the one who had made of him an apostle and had sent him out as an evangelist to the Gentiles.

Even more, so, Christ was the reward of Paul's life. The only thing that made life totally worth living was the thought that all of his life would ultimately result in Christ Himself. If Christ were to be taken from the life of

Paul, there would be nothing left. To him, Christ was nothing less than life itself.

Paul's dependency upon Christ did not end with his days of living. He made the statement, "To die is gain." Over the years this statement of Paul has frequently been misunderstood, taken out of context, and made to appear as some sick statement about life itself. This statement was not the result of any weakness on the part of Paul, but instead was the result of strength.

Paul knew that the only entrance into Christ's presence was through death. For Paul, death was not just falling asleep but an immediate entry into the presence of the Lord. For if one believes in Christ, Paul believed very strongly that death means an immediate union with Christ and with those whom we have loved and lost.

How does Paul's description of death as gain influence our gathering here in this setting? To make such a statement in this kind of setting is not some idealistic thought nor some sadistic wish. Such a position is a result of the undergirding belief in the Lord of Life.

First, death is gain because it removes us from the pain and suffering of life. Jesus, Himself, said that in this life there will be tribulation. No one is immune. We all must face those days of suffering and heartache. But when death occurs, there is not longer suffering. Death removes us from all of life's pain and suffering and ushers us into the abiding presence of Christ where there shall never again be pain.

Life includes pain and suffering. We are not promised an existence that is free from pain. Fortunately, it is all a temporary condition.

Second, death is gain because it removes us from the evils and struggles of this life. We are limited creatures. Life is most definitely a battleground between the forces of good and evil, and we are constantly caught in that battle. We are weak, and sin fills our lives, even in the best of us. There is a battle of conscience that wages itself constantly in our lives and in the lives of all believers. In fact, it is not pessimistic at all to believe that life is a long series of struggles. We grow as a result of these struggles, but they have their price.

Third, death is gain because it secures for us those things that are unfailing. Life has many disappointments. We work and strive for those things that thieves can steal, storms can destroy, and time can take away. Much of life seems to surround things that are failing. However, once we are ushered into the divine presence of Christ, all things become unfailing. For our reward shall be gifts from Christ that shall never tarnish, nor can they be taken away. They become our gifts for eternity.

Fourth, death is gain because death alone can bring us into the presence of Christ. All men and women should seek to follow the example of Paul who made Christ his ultimate goal. Christ was not only Paul's beginning, his sustaining element in life, but the end for which all of life should be lived. Christ should be our ultimate goal. To be ushered into the presence of Christ solves everything. All the problems, struggles, and pain will be done away. For the Good Shepherd of life and death will care for us in such a way that is beyond our own imagination.

Our thoughts come back to this setting. Yes, there is pain, grief, and suffering in this setting. But let us not forget the hope that surrounds us and undergirds us in this moment. For we are gathered in this setting not just to acknowledge our grief but to celebrate our hope. For with the apostle Paul, we can individually and collectively acknowledge our faith in a Lord who is in control of all of life. We recognize that death is simply the passage from one stage of life to another. Without death, our own resurrection would never be possible. Paul really was correct when he said, "For to me, to live is Christ, and to die is gain."

God give us grace to share in that kind of faith in this kind of moment.

Poem: They who on the Lord rely,
Safely dwell though danger's nigh;
Lo! His sheltering wings are spread
O'er each faithful servant's head.
When they wake, or when they sleep,
Angel guards their vigils keep;
Death and danger may be near,
Faith and love have nought to fear.
—Harriet Auber

Prayer: God, grant us the strength and courage to embrace our Faith so that we may see that all of life is in Your hands. Amen.

C. The Short Step of Death
Text: 1 Samuel 20:1-4
Focus: 1 Samuel 20:3

This particular passage contains a beautiful transaction between two dear friends: David and Jonathan. There was a covenant of friendship that embraced these two men as they determined a test to see what Saul would do next. David had been constantly running from an angry Saul. David was struggling to survive and maintain his life against this king who had set out to kill him. He had already escaped Saul's wrath on a number of occasions, but once again David found himself very close to this one who wanted to take his life. It was within this context that David made the statement, "But truly, as the Lord lives and as your soul lives, there is but a step between me and death" (1 Sam. 20:3).

It is also within this context of friendship and this covenant with Jonathan that David called upon his friend for help and companionship. And yet, one cannot overlook a certain amount of fear contained in the voice of David when he indicated, "There is but a step between me and death."

So much of our lives are spent in trying to stay ahead. We work and toil in our efforts to stay ahead of forces in life that seem to haunt us. Death is one of those forces of which we continually try to stay ahead. We think about it, we pray about it, and we consider it, both in regard to ourselves and our loved ones.

How many times do we pass close to that which could be death? As you travel on the highway, every time you pass a car you pass within inches of death. Sudden illness always bears the potential of death. No one is exempt from the fact that we are all only one breath away from death. For life is, indeed, very fragile.

David's statement reminds us all that for any of us there is a very short step—a very fine line—between life and death, at least death as we know it here on this earth.

Death is frequently something that we take for granted. There are times when we try to fool ourselves and, in our minds, push back the thought that death could ever be very close. We live and conduct ourselves as if our mortal lives would never end. But we need to recognize the truth. The truth is: there is but a short step between life and death.

Every life embraces experiences which serve to emphasize certain important facts. David was pursued by the jealous and envious Saul who hoped to push forward his kingdom by the destruction of David. David accepted this circumstance as a warning of the uncertainty of life, and he communicated his deep feelings to his friend Jonathan. It is possible that this experience which calls us together today may have brought similar warnings to us, making David's statement very appropriate to our situation. For as David said, "But truly, as the Lord lives and as your soul lives, there is but a step between me and death."

The very first thing that we must do is to

recognize the fact that life on this earth is brief. David knew that his life lay along the borderline of death at any point in time. God's Word reminds us of the same fact: "They are as a sleep: in the morning they are like grass which groweth up. In the morning it flourisheth, and groweth up; in the evening it is cut down, and withereth" (Ps. 90:5-6, KJV). The tender grass blade, the budding, the blossoming flower, shifting wind, the ever-fleeing shadow—all preach to us of the gravity and even the uncertainty of life and the certainty of death.

The delicate nature of our physical bodies tell us the very same fact. Heartbeats are messages. Our breath which may at times be silent is but a reminder that life is a gift.

Our environment with all of its negative forces remind us that life is a very fragile state. God's Word, our physical bodies, and our environment will not permit us to forget that there is, indeed, but a step between us and death.

Yet we must keep in mind that with all of these facts David did not allow the fear of death to freeze him. So it must be with our lives as well.

It is important that, as we consider death, we remember what death really is. What is that to which we approach so closely at times, yet touch only once? We can stand here today and claim promises based on God's Word that physical death does not mean annihilation. It does not mean total destruction. Death is not the end of existence.

Look at the world around us for a clue. Even nature teaches us lessons and reminds us that life goes on and on. What at first looks like the end of a cycle really is not the end of anything but the beginning of a whole new life. What looks like a dying tree and a dying plant is simply awaiting spring. What appears to be a withering flower is but awaiting a new bud. A seed will die in the earth, but a whole new plant will arise from its dying.

We do not gather here to call attention to the end of anyone's life. Instead, we come here to claim a promise that what is happening before us is not the end of anything, but the beginning of an entirely new existence that comes through the belief in our Lord Jesus Christ. It is not an exit but, rather, an entrance.

Even though one short step separates us from this thing called death, when it actually occurs, we discover that death is not what we thought. It is, indeed, so elusive! Death is not the destructive, totally mysterious force that we feared it to be. Instead, we will discover death to have been conquered already by our

Lord who experienced it for Himself, and then came back to tell us that we should not fear death because He had made preparations for us. "Let not your heart be troubled" (John 14:1).

That is why we are here today, to claim the promise made not only to our friend who has passed from this life but also to all who believe in the name of Jesus.

Even though, as David said, there may be but one step between life and death, once we experience that step we realize that it is not a giant step into the unknown. Rather, the step is a very small, short one into the arms of a loving Savior. Therefore, David's words come not as a threat but rather as a promise. That is why we are here, to celebrate the claiming of a promise made not only to this one but to each one of us as well.

Prayer: God, grant us the grace to envision all of life as within Your love. Teach us to rest upon Your promise that preparation has been made for now and eternal life. Amen.

D. The Gift of Sleep
Text: Psalm 127
Focus: Psalm 127:2

The power of Scripture is not to be found in the number of words contained in a particular passage, but the power of the promise often contained in a few words in a single verse. Such a promise is found in Psalm 127:2, and it offers a word of security to us.

We have come here to remember and to honor the memory of one called home by the Father. I stand here to remind you that in the words of the psalmist, our friend is simply sleeping. In stating these words, we are not denying the reality of death. We are not ignoring the fact that one has been called home. Death has invaded our ranks. Death is not something we can ignore. It is not emotionally healthy to deny the passing of our loved ones. God's grace is available to us for these moments, but the Holy Spirit can help us only to the degree that we are willing to recognize reality.

Therefore, the psalmist is not playing a deceptive game with us and tempting us to avoid the reality of the moment. Through the beautiful imagery of peaceful sleep, the psalmist is pointing toward the source of true rest. By use of the word *sleep*, more is implied than simply the kind of rest we take at the end of each day. We have all been tired and know of the peace of a gentle sleep. There have also been times for us when the exhaustion was so great that sleep would not come immediately. When sleep finally came, it really took on the nature of a gift. The psalmist spoke of a sleep which is needed by all who have journeyed long and hard in life.

The concept of sleep is used throughout the Bible in different ways. Old Testament Scriptures frequently refer to death when speaking of sleep (see Jer. 51:39). Not uncommon in ancient Jewish thought is the reference: "He sleeps with his fathers" to speak of death.

In the early church believers might be spoken of as those who "sleep in Jesus" when thought to have died in the faith of the Redeemer (see 1 Thess. 4:14). Jesus used the expression to describe Lazarus as sleeping: "But I go that I may wake him up" (John 11:11).

The psalmist said, "He giveth his beloved sleep" (KJV). Let us consider this sleep for a moment as we gather to honor the memory of this dear one. We need to realize that God is the Source of that gift of sleep. Certainly the sleep we receive at night can be counted as a gift. Who of us has not at some time been totally exhausted and our body cried for rest?

The sleep that came to us was a refreshing gift. There have also been times when late into the night, for whatever reason, sleep seemed never to come. When sleep finally embraced us, we counted it as a wonderful gift.

If sleep in the evening is a precious gift, so is the sleep referred to by the psalmist. Once it descends upon us, there is no more suffering, hardship, or struggle in life as we know it now. Death, with all of its mystery and unknown, is many times very merciful.

Encouraging is the fact that God not only sends sleep, but He brings it to us personally. He gently touches the eyes of His tired servants and offers the gift of sleep. The gift of sleep offered to this good friend around whose mortal body we gather is special for many reasons.

First, this sleep is special because it is inevitable and certain. Without a doubt there will come a time for each of us. We should take care not to envision this time in our lives as having been overcome or defeated. It makes more sense to see it as a time when God will cause each one of us to lie down after a busy life, and His gift to us will be restful sleep.

Second, this sleep is a special gift because of its quietness. Think of the noise of life. There are few moments when true peace exists.

Even our nightly sleep is often interrupted by a noisy world. The gift of God's sleep does indeed bring a kind of peace that in this stage of life we can only think about and imagine.

Third, this sleep is special because it represents the tenderness of God. Possibly you have been in the hospital and, due to surgery or an accident, have experienced pain. You, then, know the relief that sleep can bring. The sleep that God gives takes away the pain of suffering. God's gift of sleep is an expression of His tender love for us. He desires that we have peace.

When life and death take on the imagery of waking and sleeping we begin to see death as the natural process it is. With all of its unknowns it can be seen as a part of our inheritance. The Holy Spirit stands at our side, and the shadow of this sleep is merely the shadow of God Himself. All of the suffering, pain, and struggle are left behind. Nothing can harm the saint of God.

Death takes on the appearance of a lonely experience. This is not the case. The chambers of the dying are crowded with friends. Angels stand ready to take charge. And in the midst of all this is a gentle hand, and a soft voice which calls one from sleep. The Lord does give "His beloved sleep."

One other word needs to be said about this

sleep. Sleeping implies awakening. True is the fact that a happy awakening depends upon one's faithfulness while life's opportunities were there. What we do on earth is important. Our conduct in this life very much affects the kind of sleep that God gives. The peace of our sleep is determined by our faithfulness in this stage of life. When we awake, we will behold the face of Jesus Himself. When Lazarus awoke, the first person he beheld was Jesus. When you and I awake from this gift of sleep, the greatest joy in our lives will be to see the One who made true life possible.

These words are spoken to family and friends to remind you that what we have come here to do is not to pay homage to death. We come to celebrate God's gift of sleep. Death is not some evil force that overcomes us from behind, but is indeed a way for God to grant us the promise He has made to this loved one and to each one of us.

One of life's most difficult moments is saying good-bye to someone very special. But God gives us strength to do that when we put our faith and trust in Him. It is then we are able to see that this sleep is only a way of claiming His eternal promise.

Prayer: Lord, we entrust all our hours to

You. In our waking moments and in our sleep, we rest in You. We also entrust our loved ones to You in these moments of ultimate sleep. Amen.

E. Loneliness, Suicide, and Hope
(*For Someone Having Committed Suicide*)
Text: John 16:31-33

The reason for our gathering here is clear. We are here to give thanks for a life and to praise God, the Creator of life. We come together not because we choose to do so but because our faith demands it. Even though we gather in a spirit of worship, our hearts are so very heavy with the grief we share in common.

There is a voice within us which continues to say, *This just is not happening. Why? There is no reason to this.* The "Why?" comes because our minds are usually more logical than the world in which we live. There is a tendency for us to believe that a reason exists for everything. That belief gives us some defense against the helplessness of our existence. We seek a cause for all things, something we can comprehend and possibly control.

Indeed, one of life's most difficult challenges is to live in the midst of unanswered questions. There is, after all, so much mystery to our existence, so much we do not understand.

There are two passages of Scripture which should form the parameters of our gathering here. One is from 1 Corinthians 13:12 where Paul reminded us that we see through "a glass, darkly" (KJV). In other words, there is much that we just do not understand. Our grasp of reality is, at best, limited. Therefore, to find ourselves in the midst of circumstances we do not understand is a part of our human condition.

The second passage is from Psalm 136 where the psalmist gives thanks for God's enduring mercy. "Oh, give thanks to the Lord, for He is good! For His mercy endures forever" (v. 1). The psalmist offers comfort and hope for us today as he points to a God whose mercy is upon us. He is a God "Who remembered us in our lowly state" (v. 23). Because of God's mercy we can come together as a people of hope.

Given our setting today there are some important words that need to be spoken. In God's own time, we will know and under-

stand what is now a vast tangle of mystery and
loneliness. The passing of this one seems to be
untimely in what will continue to be a mystery. But remember that Jesus said, "Judge
not, that you be not judged. For with what
judgment you judge, you will be judged; and
with the same measure you use, it will be
measured back to you" (Matt. 7:1-2).

One thing we know, had this dear soul because of an overload of cares and responsibilities come to complete physical exhaustion
and an illness during which he/she was not
like him/herself, he/she would have been
surrounded by all with a double load of love
and care. For similar reasons, human beings
often come to deep mental problems and
even to mental collapse.

This one's passing was no more or no less
due to sickness than if death had resulted
from some other cause. It was death due to
illness just as much as if death had been due
to heart failure or cancer.

There was suffering in this one's life. Suffering is a part of life. None of us can answer why
people must suffer and die. In different ways
and at different times, we must all suffer. For
reasons that will remain a mystery in this life,
this one's life had become one of pain. There
was distress that seemed larger than life. And
there is no way for us to explain it. We cannot

get into another person's mind. For whatever reason, life became unbearable.

As family you should take caution not to become overwhelmed with guilt that all of this is the result of something you did or did not do. If death occurred from incurable cancer, you could not have changed the direction of events. Even so here the same is true.

Only an Eternal God can know the sickness and suffering which can grip both mind and spirit. But God does know. We only must endeavor to remember the goodness and kindness which characterized this one's life. The rest we must safely leave to the Father's love and mercy.

Our challenge at this point is to turn to God and to Christ Jesus, our Savior, for comfort and assurance. As Jesus faced what appeared to be certain death He said, "Behold the hour cometh, yea, is now come, that ye shall be scattered, every man to his own, and shall leave me alone: and yet I am not alone, because the Father is with me" (John 16:32, KJV).

I bring this to your attention because I believe that Jesus is saying now to you whose shock has turned to bewilderment and grief, "You are not alone, for the Father is with you."

Therefore, the real question for us today is

not "Why?" but "How?" Now that this has happened, how may we face it? How may we find strength to face our pain and grief, and still go on affirming life and the God who gives it?

We are not protected from life's pain. God does not prevent our suffering, and yet He does not cause it. Instead, He meets us in the midst of life, even here today as He has always met us, with a love that goes to a cross. Only in that faith and hope can we continue to move forward. We come together today to share our faith and our hope. We do it in the midst of our tears and unanswered questions.

In these moments of loneliness, remember the symbolic embrace of friends of our common faith. Most of all remember the words of Jesus, "I am not alone, because the Father is with Me." Christ found comfort in this truth. In this same truth, your comfort is to be found.

Prayer: Our Father, there is much to life that we do not understand. We "see through a glass, darkly." Until that which is partial disappears, we will trust in You. Embrace our loved one with Your merciful arms of love. We offer our prayer in the name of One who came as Ultimate Love. Amen.

F. The Lord Gives and Takes
Text: Job 1:19-21
Focus: Job 1:21

The possibility exists for you to misunderstand me when I say that there is a rhythm to life. The misunderstanding may occur if you assume that I believe the world operates totally as a cycle. History is not cyclical but linear. Life is an unfolding saga that is moving into the future under the all-powerful eyes of God. History is being influenced by God; therefore, we are not victims of a repetitive cycle.

Yet even a casual observation of life indicates that a certain rhythm prevails in our existence. This rhythm does not signify the absence of God but is an indication of God's love as He provides predictability to life. Our gathering here today is a part of that rhythm.

Our text refers to a man who knew well all aspects of life. He also knew that there was a rhythm to life that included good and bad, joy and laughter, life and death. In swift succession Job had lost his property and his children. Yet in the midst of his great loss, Job was able to rely on his faith in God and say, "The Lord gave, and the Lord has taken away;/Blessed be the name of the Lord" (1:21). There is a divine rhythm of give and take to life. The Lord gives, and the Lord takes away. In this setting we would agree that all life is a gift of God. Our daily existence is a reminder of the gracious gifts of our loving God. Our own life as well as life all about us is not the evolvement of matter or a result of some cosmic accident. We are persons created in the image of God. We have purpose and design from the uncreated One. Job said, "The Lord gave." What does He give? Obviously, this physical life we enjoy and yearn to maintain is a gift of God.

God also adds quality to this physical life. Happiness is a gift from God. Even now you recall many hours of happiness with this our departed loved one and friend. Happiness does add a quality to life. Happiness makes everything better. God gave us happiness that we might be better people. Memories of happy events continue to warm us and motivate us.

In this memorial service, there is another gift of God which we should not overlook. Saint Paul said, "Thanks be unto God for his unspeakable gift" (2 Cor. 9:15, KJV). That unspeakable gift is the salvation made possible through Christ Jesus. God's gift of salvation through His Son as the Savior of the world is what makes life worthwhile. It is that which gives us such joy. The gift of salvation allows our setting today to become a type of celebration. Salvation is God's gift to dry our tears, to lift the burden of death from our hearts, and to comfort all who mourn. Death would be an unbearable experience were it not for God's gift. There is hope.

We must come back to Job. He also said, "The Lord has taken away." We have hardly listed all these gifts from God when we are reminded of this setting. God has taken away. There are many losses in life, but now comes the greatest loss. The Lord has taken a loved one, and death has invaded a family.

A loved one has been taken. If we truly believe that He created life, we must confess that He has the right to do with life as He so chooses. Through this life of our friend He has shared a precious gift, and now He has called that life home.

In the process of doing so, the appearance is that God has taken back His second gift: happiness. No one expects you to be happy when saying good-bye to someone who is very special. Because God has been with us in Christ, He knows the sorrow of losing a loved one.

It is easy to be trapped and misled into believing that there is no happiness in death. We are primarily aware of tears and troubled hearts. We may even wonder if God has forgotten us. Then we remember His third gift which He has never recalled and suddenly everything begins to look different. As we remember the gift of salvation, hope shines through the gloom. Even though God has called home a life and tears are real, in Christ Jesus we have a salvation that is steadfast and sure. Overarching and undergirding our gathering here is the fact of salvation.

If we see through the eyes of our faith, we can join Job and say, "Blessed be the name of the Lord." While the appearance is that physical life and happiness have been taken back, salvation through Christ Jesus has not been recalled. The Lord gives, but He does not take all His gifts back.

We must remember that all of life is in the hands of God. Faith will overcome grief which flows from the rhythm of our days. Through strength from our faith we can say with Job, "The Lord gave, and the Lord has taken away."

Because we are human, we grieve here and now. May we show the confidence of our faith by our personal testimony as we say, "Blessed be the name of the Lord."

Prayer: Lord, You have given, and now You have taken from us. Even in our grief and pain, we continue to call You "Blessed." For giving us the life of this dear soul and the gift of many memories, we offer our thanks. Most of all, for the gift of eternal life which is never taken away, we offer our thanks. In Christ's name, Amen.

G. Our Strength and Resting Place
Text: Psalm 46
Focus: Psalm 46:11

One would be hard pressed to find stronger words of comfort than those found in Psalm 46. These words, though written long ago, provide a sense of security for troubled times, even moments such as these.

We have come to this place today for a very important purpose, that we might openly acknowledge our love for a very special person. We have also come together to openly acknowledge our support for this family. For your loss and your pain, we can offer no quick remedies or answers, only our concern, our thoughts, and our prayers.

In times like these, we are fortunate to have the Word of God as a resource. The Word has stood the test of time, and it has been proven true by our own experience. Psalm 46 speaks to that which is being felt right here today.

Let us get past the language of the Psalms and hear the powerful message. We do not know exactly to what the psalmist was responding when he wrote these words. Some powerful force obviously made him feel very weak and afraid. Whatever it was, the force was very powerful because he spoke of the mountains being carried into the sea, the waters roaring, and the earth trembling.

The psalmist felt helpless on his own strength. Possibly during these past hours you have identified with his sense of helplessness. How helpless we feel when we want life for someone! We would do anything to change the course of events, and yet there appears to be little, if anything, we can do to redirect the inevitable.

The psalmist evidently knew the feeling well. Some have thought that there was a foreign army invading the land destroying as it went. Others have felt that it was some catastrophe of nature, a flood, or an earthquake. Whatever the problem may have been, whether some catastrophe of nature or the terror of some invading army, the psalmist had found the manifestation of the splendor of the Lord of Hosts even in terror.

Yet in the midst of all this terror, his faith allowed him to stand strong, and even above all of the noise, he was able to hear the still, quiet voice of God. There was no doubt in his mind that God was still in control of the world and that He was indeed a source of strength and refuge. Even as you gather today there may be questions in your mind about God's control of our world. In order to hear, the psalmist had to first be still. "Be still, and know that I am God: I will be exalted among the heathen, I will be exalted in the earth" (v. 10, KJV).

Now, these who have suffered the loss of this loved one also find themselves in a similar time. There are no mountains being visibly carried into the sea, but in a very strange way, the earth is trembling, and we find ourselves under the influence of a very powerful force. We know very little about this force of death, one that very quickly puts us in touch with our limited capacities as human beings. Now, there is a different kind of insecurity, but we can hear the quiet voice of God if we only allow ourselves to be still. "The Lord of hosts is with us; the God of Jacob is our refuge" (v. 11 KJV).

There are needs which are very evident

today, and the God of this psalmist is the same God at work in our modern world. He is our Source of refuge and strength. His strength can help us bridge the change which has suddenly overwhelmed us. We need God's unchanging nature in a world that is constantly changing and, at times, may bring with it experiences of pain.

What does the psalm about God, the Conqueror of the nations, have to do with grief? It has everything to do with it. Grief shakes us at our deepest level. Grief creates fear. Our world may appear to be turned upside down. In the midst of this trouble, God comes in strength and offers refuge and strength. God not only helps us: He is a present help.

The God of Jacob, our God, is above and beyond all things. "He uttered His voice, the earth melted" (v. 6). By speaking a single word, He can change the appearance of all things. There is no circumstance in our life beyond God's ability to help.

There are few times in our lives when we need strength and refuge more than when death invades our ranks. There is no need for panic, no need for frenzied efforts for survival, and certainly no need to give up. Only one act is needed: "Be still, and know that I am God;/I will be exalted among the nations,/I will be exalted in the earth!/The Lord of hosts is with us;/The God of Jacob is our refuge" (vs. 10-11).

Prayer: Our Father, we need a source of strength and refuge. We need a resting place. For being this kind of help in time of trouble, we offer our thanks. Bless the memory of this dear one. Grant us all the peace that comes from trusting in You. Amen.

H. God Loves All Children
(*For a Child Dead Soon After Birth*)
Text: 2 Samuel 12:15-23

The setting of grief is difficult enough under normal circumstances. There is a tendency for us to justify the death of someone who has lived a long and full life. Though unspoken, feelings exist that such a person's life has come full circle. They have worked hard, served well, and now the time has come to lay down and rest. Death comes as a gentle sleep to a mature soul who has been faithful in life. Even under these circumstances grief brings pain and sadness.

How much more difficult it is to accept and

explain the death of one whose life must be measured by minutes rather than years. A multitude of questions come to our minds, and most of these center around the age-old question: "Why?" Most of these questions will remain unanswered, at least for this segment of life's journey.

The wisdom of God's Word will lead us away from the "Why?" question and point us toward the "What?" question. The temptation is to become bogged down in the "Whys" of this event while the real issue is: What do we now do under these circumstances?

There is a story recorded in 2 Samuel which offers a great deal of wisdom for this moment: an experience of David as he dealt with the death of his child by Bathsheba. Granted, there were some rather peculiar circumstances surrounding the birth of this child. David had brought about this child under conditions that were less than honorable. Yet the wisdom offered through this experience is not the manner in which the child was conceived, but the way David dealt with the child's death.

The fact must be emphasized that David loved the child. His pain due to the child's death was intense. While his spiritual maturity can be questioned in the child's conception, there can be no question about his maturity concerning the death of the child.

Consider David's experience. Bathsheba gave birth to the child. The child became very sick. When David learned of the child's illness, he begged that the child be spared. Scripture indicates that David fasted and lay all night on the bare earth.

The leaders of the nation became very concerned and begged him to get up and eat with them. David refused. On the seventh day the baby died, and David's aides were afraid to tell him. They were concerned about what he might do to himself when he heard the news. He seemed to be so upset already.

David heard them whispering and was wise enough to know what had happened. What David did at this point is very significant. Instead of losing control as they expected, David did just the opposite. He took complete control of himself, got up, bathed, brushed his hair, changed his clothes, and went to the Temple to worship God. David's aides were astonished when he returned to the palace and ate. When questioned about his behavior, David said that he had prayed and fasted that God would let the child live. Yet the child died, and now life must go on.

Note that David went to God in prayer and fasting. He prayed that the child would live.

We are always free to go to God. Prayer was David's lifeline. In past days you have become familiar with such a process. You have prayed that this child would be spared. You have taken your petitions to God, and you should! Prayer is our lifeline.

Yet, in spite of the prayer, it did not work out for you. Life has much for us that we cannot explain. Our trust in God is not a guarantee that life will always work out as we desire. God's ways are beyond us. Life cannot be figured out. Life is not a game we play.

The strength of David's character came through at this point. Obviously, the acceptance of the circumstances was not easy, and it seldom is. Notice, however, that David did not let the circumstances alienate him from God. We observe David as he obviously felt that life now must go on. Indeed, life must go on, and life did for David.

In some ways this experience of David reflects our setting here. You prayed that it would work out. You were seeking happiness, and I believe God wants you to be happy.

At first, David was reluctant to accept reality. Not one of us wants to hear bad news. We do not understand all that has happened here. Most importantly, however, you must not see this as God's punishment. The God we worship does not kill babies to punish adults!

Like David, your life must go on. Life must continue. It cannot stop here. God has a future for you and your family. Your future begins right now as you move out from this moment. As with David, you must continue to trust in God and His wisdom. Life does not stop here. There are other experiences which call us forward. We do ourselves and our Lord an injustice when we become angry at the lack of answers to our "Whys" and become immobile.

Even now we must take our case to God. He will give us strength not only to bear up but to move on from this place. Life must go on. We must take that which we cannot change and move into a future which is secure and which shall become happy again.

Yet, happiness may seem so far away. You, too, have lain all night before God. Now with God's strength you will pick yourself up, wash yourself and your clothes, and move into the future. We do not have to understand life, only return to it. God's strength is offered for this moment. Sufficient is God's strength for our needs. Pain is real, but so is God's grace.

Prayer: Take our pain and disappointment and fill the vacuum with Your power and love. Remind us that happiness comes not from answered

"Whys" but from trust in Your merciful love. Amen.

I. Suffering and God's Grace
(*For One Having Suffered Long*)
Text: 2 Corinthians 12:7-10)

We cannot escape the fact that life involves
the extremes of joy and sadness, laughter and
tears, pleasure and suffering. As we gather in
this setting today, one side of the scale seems
most prevalent. Momentarily, the joy is cov-
ered by the sadness. Tears have washed away
the laughter. And this gathering seems to conclude a long journey of suffering. One of the
challenges of this moment is to realize that
joy, laughter, and pleasure have not been per-
manently destroyed. In God's grace they will
return. As the author of Revelation has stated,
"God will wipe away every tear from their
eyes; there shall be no more death" (Rev. 21:-
3-4).

The journey of suffering is not an easy one.
This good friend, whom we come today to
remember, knew well this experience. This
one could empathize with Paul who spoke
freely about his own suffering. In the elev-

enth chapter of 2 Corinthians Paul listed the five times he received forty stripes minus one from the Jews, and occasions when he was beaten three times with rods, stoned once, and shipwrecked three times.

However, the worst of Paul's suffering came from his thorn in the flesh. We do not know what his "thorn" was, and it really does not matter. We only know that it caused him great suffering and pain. Scripture indicates that he pleaded three times with the Lord to remove this source of suffering (v. 8). This aspect of his life was not a game to Paul but a very serious matter.

The response of God to Paul's pleas has become a source of hope for all who have spent endless hours in the night with pain. The response of God was and continues to be: "My grace is sufficient for you" (v. 9). Our first impression might be that God had not taken the plea of Paul very seriously. Yet even our own experience teaches that God addressed the problem with the only true solution.

Paul understood his circumstances as a way of making him open to Christ's strength. He knew firsthand the meaning of dependency upon God, and his experience of suffering actually became an asset to his faith rather than a liability.

For us today, there is the question that

comes from deep within us: Why did God not heal Paul? Why did God not heal this friend? There certainly was no shortage of prayers offered in his behalf. These are questions that for the present must remain unanswered, and no one can speak for God. Yet, there is one claim that can be made with all certainty, and it is that God takes no pleasure in the suffering of any of His children. Upon that claim you can rest your faith.

God is no sadist. The God we worship cries with us in our pain. In all circumstances of life, He is at work for good. As does any earthly father, God wants His children to be happy and healthy. Then, why does God not bring healing immediately? We simply do not have those answers.

It would appear that the strength of Paul's character came from the weathering of storms. His suffering became for him the source of spiritual strength. I cannot help but think of this aspect of Paul's life when I think of this one we honor today. There was a thorn in the flesh. This one struggled with that thorn as best as possible, and it would appear on the surface that the struggle ended as a loss. But, I remind you that "we see through a glass, darkly" (1 Cor. 13:12, KJV).

This I do know: suffering was not an indication of God's punishment. Once Jesus with

His disciples encountered a blind man. His disciples asked who sinned to bring about the blindness. Jesus refused to point a finger at anyone's sin as an explanation.

Our friend's suffering and death was not the result of anyone's sin. The multitude of questions that arise must simply remain a mystery for now. Someday we will see though a glass that is clear; and we will know in full, not in part. Until then, we have no choice but to move on and trust in a God who has all answers and all wisdom. As family and friends today, you are not exempt from suffering. Grief has turned your joy into sadness and your laughter into tears. You know even in this moment the pain that life can offer.

We need security, warmth, and assurance. There is a source available. God's strength is sufficient for our needs now as it will be in all other circumstances of life. Consider the image of comfort offered in Isaiah 40:10-11. The image is a very warm picture of God's love that embraces. "He will feed." "He will gather." "[He will] carry them in His bosom." He will do all of this not just in the good and easy days but in the difficult days as well.

I cannot tell you why good people suffer. I cannot tell you why people become ill and even die. For Paul, our friend, and Isaiah, God came in strength during moments of weakness.

Isaiah went on to say that all of this is not in vain. God does come to those who wait. This one did a full share of waiting, and so have you. At the point of what seems to be failing strength, God gives power to the faint. Because of faithful waiting there has been a great reversal. After a long descent of growing weary, God has kept His promise, and all has been changed. Because of God's presence and power, we will all once again soar like eagles, run and not be weary, walk and not faint (see Isa. 40:31).

For our beloved, that change has taken place. The claiming of Isaiah's promise has taken place even as we gather in this place. That ought to be a source of comfort in the midst of grief for each of us.

As you remember this friend and loved one, let the good memories be a source of warmth for you. There is so much good to be tucked away.

For this one there is no more pain, no more suffering, only joy and peace. For each of us, God's strength is sufficient.

Prayer: God, give us the strength to rest securely in Your grace. In the midst of grief and pain, Your strength is sufficient for all of life. In our Lord's name, we offer this prayer. Amen.

J. The Shining Light of the Just
(*For an Aged Mother*)
Text: Proverbs 4:18

There are many translations of this verse, but none is as replete with imagery as the King James translation. "The path of the just is as the shining light, that shineth more and more unto the perfect day" (Prov. 4:18) How appropriate for our setting here!

Not one of us is here without bearing the influence of special persons in our lives. It has been said that no man is an island, and it is true. We cannot even debate the issue. The only question is in what ways do we show forth this influence. If we are influenced daily by our contacts with people in general, how much more are we touched by those close to us?

How grateful we should be for those strong persons who have preceded us and hopefully have made impressions upon us. Few people have the power of influence upon us as do our mothers. She has touched our lives in ways

beyond our counting. Her influence at times
has been subtle and quiet. There have been
other times when it has been as bold and obvious as the thunder. Her light has been upon
our path since the moment of our first breath,
and that influence will continue uninterrupt-
ed even by this grave. How much we owe
those who have cast light upon our path! And
how we need that light! Otherwise, darkness
can be overwhelming.

A hunter tells the story of hunting deer
with a friend in unfamiliar woods. The path
was clear in the light of the sun. The two were
to meet before dark at an obvious and specified place in the woods before returning to
the truck. The unfamiliar hunter was overwhelmed by the beauty of the woods. The
colors were bright, the wind was crisp, and
the birds all sang in concert. Hunting became
secondary to the beauty of the moment.

The sun began to set, but the hunter was so
intrigued by nature that he wanted to wait
until the last moment. But dark came so suddenly. In what seemed like seconds, the colors
turned to darkness, and all the animals
became quiet. The path which had been so
clear only minutes before became totally in-
distinct. After a few turns, the direction of the
meeting place was completely lost, and suddenly the darkness became overwhelming.

The woods were too thick to determine a path. There was nowhere to go. The hunter was at the mercy of the night.

After a while the sound of whistling could be heard. A beam of light could be seen like a flare. Of course, it was the friend who had guessed the problem and, with the aid of a flashlight, had come to offer guidance through a dark path. Thanks to the friend and his light, the path became clear and, in minutes, both were in the truck and on the way home.

The hunter's experience has been relived many times in everyone's life. The time of darkness was probably not in the woods, but darkness takes many forms. Throughout our lives, we need someone to come to us and offer light to our path.

Who has offered more light to our journey than our mothers? And her influence has been even more powerful when the light she brought was none other than Christ, our Lord. She has offered not only herself but the Source of all light.

Therefore, our gathering here is a tender hour. Yet, in no way is this an hour of tragedy. It is appropriate that we honor the passing of this one who has lived long and full. We honor one who has offered kindness and love and loyalty to Christ in her life.

Let us see this hour as it is meant to be, not a time of darkness but another time when she brings light. This moment is a time of grief, but let us not dwell on loss. Instead, let us grasp the measure of our gratitude for this life lived before us.

Particularly appropriate to this occasion are the words of the Scripture just read. Indeed, she has been one of the just, and her pathway has been a shining light.

If a light is to help us, we must stand in its light, or we shall continue to stumble. Long ago, this dear lady faced that light and set her feet upon the pathway of the just. The light she discovered was not to be possessed but shared. Through her faith she has shared that light and offered direction to the dark paths of others.

Like all journeys, this pilgrimage of hers came to an end. Yet she knew she was in God's keeping, and the end of her path was only a shadow. Such was her faith and comfort, and so is ours to be found. Because of this fine lady, your heritage is a most valuable one. Yours is the memory of a good mother whom you can always remember, love, and respect. Her life has been light for your path, and her death shall not conclude that influence. She waits for you, and the pathway to her has been illumined by her life and love.

Where do you go from here? Very quickly, let me conclude by making a few suggestions.

1. Claim her memory. Memories are gifts from God. Yours is a good one, a very special one. Let it warm you, motivate you, lift you, and let it make you laugh as well as make you cry.

2. Claim your heritage. Yours is a rich one. Any money left is not even a part of it. The heritage she leaves is much more: love, respect, honor, integrity, and a good name.

3. Let her go. Release her. That is a real challenge. God has promised to comfort us, but the Holy Spirit can heal our grief only to the point we are willing to release our loved ones into the arms of a God we say we trust. You must give her up. That is tough, but it is the only option that makes sense.

4. Move on from this moment. The women who came to Jesus' tomb found the stone rolled away. The angel asked, "Why do you seek the living among the dead?" (Luke 24:5c). It was another way of saying, "Don't stand here, get on with the business at hand." The work to which each of us is called must go on.

The writer of proverbs was right on target.

"The path of the just is as the shining light" (KJV).

Prayer: Oh God, we thank You for the light of Your Son and the way that light has shone through the love of our mothers. Amen.

K. To Remember, Comfort, and Claim
Text: 1 Thessalonians 4:13-18
Focus: 1 Thessalonians 4:13

Paul may have had many reasons for writing the words contained in the fourth chapter of 1 Thessalonians, but surely one of his primary intents was to admonish the Thessalonians to comfort one another. He offered instruction concerning a matter about which someone had evidently inquired. We have little information regarding the way the problem arose other than what is implied in the passage.

Apparently, the Thessalonian Christians had anticipated the second coming of the Lord and were concerned about those disciples who had passed away. They were anxious about the relation of the dead in Christ to the

Lord's coming. Paul's answer to their concern was that those who had died would share equally with those who were still alive. The words which Paul offered in that day long ago remain a source of comfort and strength for us even in this setting today.

Consider the purpose of our gathering. We have not assembled to quickly move through some hollow ritual. Instead, there are several very important reasons why we are here. Allow me a few minutes to mention only three.

First we have come here to remember a fine Christian. It is good to remember because our minds are gifts from God. Our memories warm us in moments of loneliness. Our memories help us in moments of decision.

Together we claim the memory of this friend's investment in our lives. Memories of loved ones are not taken with the passing of their mortal bodies. Consider the influence of this one. Through memory, that influence shall continue.

As we walk with people we are shaped by them. The good in one person can easily become the good of another. Some of you can honestly say that some of the good in your life is because of this one whose memory we claim today. Our memory is truly a gift of God and can be the source of great joy. Certainly you will cherish the memory of this dear one. That is the way it should be.

There is a second reason why we have come together today. We are here to offer comfort and support. The work of grief is never an easy task. Pain is a part of our human experience, especially within the context of personal loss. Jesus understood that part of our humanity. He said, "Blessed are they that mourn: for they shall be comforted" (Matt. 5:4).

Through Christ, our Lord, we offer support to one another in this setting. One of the values of the incarnation is that God knows and understands because He has been here. At this very moment He knows your pain and can help. Without the incarnation there might be doubt in our minds that God really does understand our pain just now.

Therefore, we come together to offer support to a grieving family and friends. That support is very important. Moving through this kind of experience without the aid of the Christian community must be difficult.

Family, you will continue to be lifted in our prayers as you adjust to the change in your lives created by the passing of this dear one.

If our reasons ended here, there would be sadness indeed, and the sorrow would be overwhelming. But there is an even greater reason for gathering here. Most of all, we come together to claim our hope, not some vague fantasy but hope based upon fact. The resurrection of our Lord adds a dimension to the event of death that will never be erased. Consider again the words of Paul. He did not want us to be ignorant about death. He wanted us today to know what he had already discovered.

We are not to sorrow as those who have no hope. From the human perspective, death is an awesome thing. Death is powerful, mysterious, and frightening. If death had the final word, this moment would be a time of nothing but grief. But this is not the end. This dear one around whose mortal body we gather has experienced a change. Death is a passage from one life to another. This one has claimed the promise, a promise made to each one of us.

Christianity is founded on hope. The simple and great truth about Jesus is hope. For that reason, the gospel is good news. This hope is grounded in what Paul declared in verse 14. Our hope is the resurrection of Christ. If Christ is not risen, then our hope is in vain.

This is the gospel that the world needs today. This gospel so desperately needed by the world is the gospel of hope, the gospel of

Christ whose creative power is capable of lifting us above any and all things which come at us from so many directions.

Out of the resurrection hope comes a new attitude toward death. Death just is not the same as it was. The whole concept of immortality is beyond us to comprehend. We only have to claim it.

We come back to where we started—this admonition of Paul concerning the hope that is a part of our believers' inheritance. We should not sorrow as those who have no hope. "For if we believe that Jesus died and rose again, even so God will bring with Him those who sleep in Jesus" (v. 14).

Therefore, we come together to remember —to remember a fine Christian individual. We come together to individually and collectively offer support in a time of grief and sadness.

But, most of all, we gather to claim our hope—hope that is found in a loving God who sent His Son that none should perish. Let hope embrace us as we move from this place.

Prayer: O God, without hope we could not exist. Life would be unbearable. But because of Jesus, we have a hope that takes us not only through this present crisis but also through all of

life. Thank You for the hope that is
ours in the life, death, and resurrection of Your Son. In whose name we
approach You. Amen.

L. The Death of His Saints
(*For the Saintly Woman*)
Text: Psalms 116:1-15
Focus: Psalms 116:15

There are some statements in Holy Scripture which, if taken out of context, might
seem contrary to human thinking. The biblical concept of death might be an example of
such. To most of us death is equated with sorrow and tears. This event is understood by
society as a time of great anxiety. The fear of
death is commonly so great that we anticipate
it and all of its emotion long before it actually
occurs.

Most of us instinctively avoid even the dis-
cussion of death, for within every heart lurks
the fear of death and dying. We prefer not to
talk about it. We do not like to think about it.
Deep within us, death appears to be the ultimate defeat.

God, however, takes a decidedly different
view of death. In His Word God says that

death can be precious. The particular verse upon which we have focused our attention is taken from a context of thanksgiving. As we read the psalm we can envision one who had come to the Temple to offer a vow and a sacrifice. It is obvious that at some point he had suffered affliction and in his hour of need he had taken a vow that if the Lord delivered him he would make a pilgrimage to the Temple and offer appropriate sacrifices. We do not know the nature of his affliction, only that it was serious.

In keeping his vows, the psalmist had done more than just offer a temporary sacrifice. There is implied in the psalm the willingness of the psalmist to submit himself totally to God. He prayed and desired deliverance, but he rendered his own will to that of God to the point that death may be seen as within the precious and loving arms of God.

In the submission of his own will to that of God, the psalmist's concept of death took on a quality that was and continues to be inconceivable by the secular world. He is joyful in God's delivering his soul from death but totally at peace with death as well, for all takes place within the sight of the Lord.

Yet the fact must be acknowledged that only a person of saintly character could offer this kind of vow. Only one who has lived a life close to God can approach death from this different perspective.

For the saints of God, death is one of those areas where there is a distinct advantage over those who have never exercised that faith. Through the eyes of our faith, death takes on an unusual quality. God says that death can be precious, and more so than just relieving pain.

There are inevitable questions which people will ask concerning the scriptural assertion that death can be a precious thing. To whom is it precious? The text indicates that it is precious to God.

Death is not a precious thing to the physician. To a degree it indicates defeat because medical science could not change the inevitable. Death is also not too precious to those left behind. The pain of separation is real. Yet to the saints of God, death is but a natural completion of a journey begun long ago.

Death is a way of allowing God to exercise His wisdom and love. His thoughts are above us, and His ways are beyond us. The saints have learned the secret of happiness by letting God be God, even in regard to the taking of our own lives and the lives of our loved ones.

Yet death is precious to God only in the lives of certain people. One can assume that not every life represents a successful molding process. Not everyone walks the road with God. Death becomes a terrifying experience for those who have never seen the light of the cross.

These words do not suggest that death is a game which our Lord plays to occupy His time. Neither is death a means of meeting His own divine needs. The text, instead, suggests that God takes our lives seriously. There is not one single aspect of our lives which is omitted from God's care. Life is a gift, and, therefore, one's death is a valued concern of God. Truly precious in the sight of the Lord is the death of His saints. Why is this true? Because death marks the completion of something God began long ago. Not one life is an accident. He sends every life into the world for the purpose of molding that life until ready for eternal life with God. For the saint, death marks the completion of that process. Death may be seen as God now considering the life ready for even greater things. Death suddenly becomes a time of celebration. God's work in that life has been completed.[1]

Does this Scripture not provide a backdrop for our gathering today? The life of this one was no accident. She was a part of God's plan. The beauty of her experience may be found in the fact that successful molding has taken place. God has sent His angel to tap this good lady on the shoulder and say that she has done a good job. Essentially, we are here to celebrate a job well done. That is a cause for joy, not sadness.

This is a time for thanksgiving—not for what has been taken but for what has been given. Consider the gifts that are left behind as an inheritance.

First, she has left a good name. There is no shame for you here. We have sometimes made pride seem shameful. Yet there is a kind of pride that is special: a good name.

Second, she has left behind a good example. She was as human as the rest of us, but let's face it—some just have a better grip on life's realities than others do. There was no question as to the priorities in her life.

Third, she has left you the assurance of being loved. You, family and friends as well, have an advantage over many people. Many people live a lifetime without experiencing the love you have received from her.

Her death becomes a way of your claiming these gifts, and because of that inheritance you discover that her passing has become a precious thing for you as well.

We come back to the words of the psalmist. He had submitted his entire life to the will of God. Therefore, every phase of life had significance. Most especially was this true concerning death. Death is not the ultimate defeat for the believer. Instead, it is the successful completion of a project begun long ago. Death is not the revoking of life but the gentle touch of the Creator who says, "Come with me, and let's celebrate a job well done."

The statement really is true: "Precious in the sight of the Lord/Is the death of His saints" (v. 15).

Prayer: Father God, enable us to claim the gifts left behind by this dear lady. Most of all help us to envision our own lives as a project with You. Give us grace to live our days in such a way that our lives and our deaths may be precious in Your sight. Amen.

Note

1. Charles L. Wallis, ed., *The Funeral Encyclopedia* (Grand Rapids: Baker Book House, 1953), p. 120.

M. The Real Measure of Success
(*For the Saintly Man*)
Texts: Psalm 90:10, Revelation 22:14

Why is it that when we hear of the death of someone, we frequently ask about their age? If we hear of a friend's parent passing away, our first question will frequently be, "How old was he?" When a friend's work associate dies, sooner or later we get around to asking, "How old was he?" or, "How old was she?"

Perhaps one reason we ask is that it seems to be easier to justify in our minds the death of someone more advanced in years. If one has accumulated enough years we can more easily accept one's death and assume it to be a natural event. Death seems less tragic when we can say they had a "full life."

The concern for one's age is obviously a result of the fact that we tend to measure one's life in years as though that were the sole gauge. The success of human life depends largely on how it is measured.

The psalmist stated, "The days of our years are three-score years and ten" (Ps. 90:10, KJV). In doing so, he had only given us a description of life's expectancy. We do not have a guarantee for that many years. We can all name persons who never came close to that age, and we can think of some who have far exceeded that number. The psalmist was only saying that the average life expectancy is seventy years, and, even then, when compared to God, these years are but a sign (see Ps. 90:9).

We have come here to remember one who accumulated many years. And yet his life can be measured in many ways. First, his life can be measured in years, and certainly that is a very natural thing to do. There is no shame in accumulating time. One half of all born in the world die in infancy and childhood. Of those who reach ten, only two out of five reach threescore and ten. One in a hundred reaches ninety, and one in a hundred thousand lives a full century.[1]

With the advances in medical science, human duration is becoming longer. Yet our mortal bodies remain subject to stress and age; therefore, we must continue to deal with the fact that time runs out.

There are other ways of measuring life than age. Consider the accomplishments of an individual. Some people do far more with a few years than many do with a large number. A life especially worth celebrating is one who combines numbers of years and accomplishments. Keep in mind that life's true accomplishments are not always the ones which appear in the newspaper headlines. Most great acts of love go unnoticed by the masses. In fact, many labors of love are known only by God.

It is unfortunate that the normal measure of a life values quantity over quality. Consider the life of our Lord. You cannot question the quality of His life, and what He did in a small number of years. Consider the one around whom we gather in memorial here. The quality of his life will be remembered long after the quantity.

There is still yet another measure. Some are remembered only in terms of the circumstances under which they lived. For example, consider the changes that have occured in the lifetime of this dear one. So much has changed. In science, world events, and culture there is little about our world that is the same as when he was young.

Yet most changes in circumstances occur beyond our control. We may have little or nothing to do with revolutionary events in our lifetime. While we may be remembered for having lived in a certain era of history, we can claim little credit for it.

Another measure exists which must not be forgotten. Our most important measure is at the point of preparation for life to come. In fact, the best way to live this life is in preparation for the life to follow. One lives best who early chooses the only true foundation for life. All other measures become insignificant by comparison.

Preparation for life beyond is a lifelong process. This preparation is not a crash course in eternal survival occuring at the last minute. The preparation begins the moment one opens oneself to salvation through Christ as Lord. Preparation for life beyond continues through all of one's days. When that moment of death comes in the history of each one of us, the event becomes a simple transition.

The writer of Revelation has stated it well, "Blessed are those who do His commandments, that they may have the right to the tree of life, and may enter through the gates into the city" (Rev. 22:14).

In one sense our celebration of this one's life comes from all of these measures. There has been an accumulation of years. There have been personal accomplishments. The historical circumstances in which his life was lived were momentous. But the most important measure is recorded in terms of preparation. He took seriously this mortal life, and he never forgot the life that will endure the storms of time and the fires of judgment. His preparation for life was complete.

Both the psalmist and the writer of Revelation described the mortal life of our departed friend. Yes, his days were threescore and ten; but, more importantly, he has kept the commandments. He has been given the right to the tree of life and now has entered through the gates of the city. That event is worthy of our celebration.

Prayer: God, give us grace to consider the way our lives are being measured. May the life of this our treasured friend remind us never to ignore the quality of life at the expense of quantity. We ask our prayer in the name of our Perfect Example. Amen.

Note

1. Erdman, ed., *60 Funeral Messages*, (Grand Rapids: Baker Book House, 1979), p. 9.

N. "God and the Natural Order"
Text: Ecclesiastes 3:1-8
Focus: Ecclesiastes 3:6

These particular verses are read by ministers as a background for many situations and may seem rather strange to offer them in this setting. On the contrary, they are most appropriate. This particular section of Ecclesiastes was probably written as a chant and has lost some of the rhythm in translation.

The passage describes much of what we do in the process of living. All of these activities are within the range of normal human endeavor—what people do or leave undone. One may also find here a suggestion of the variety of experiences of life.

Life is not one simple activity. Life involves thesis and its antithesis. Here is a reminder that there is a time for loss as well as a time for gain. There are moments of laughter and moments of tears. Life is a mixture of the bright and the dark. The wise person will learn to accept the light as well as the shadows. This is a part of God's natural order.

Verse 7 speaks directly to our setting here. When the writer spoke of rending, he was thought by some to be referring to the ritual act of tearing the clothing in times of sorrow or mourning. Emotion is a part of grief, and it must find expression.

The antithetical line that follows refers to keeping silent. There are times when our sorrow must be silent. Grief is a long process, and quiet hours are a part of the journey.

We gather here today in memorial to one who has known all of these experiences. Within that life has vibrated the wisdom of God's natural order. Obviously, there was a time to be born, and now there is a time to die. In the meantime, consider all that our friend has witnessed. Just think of the changes that have occurred within the natural order of his life. There have been many times of casting away and many times of gathering in.

But the routine and order does not rule out God's working and weaving His purpose into every life.

This dear one was no accident, and neither is his passing from us. There is a time to be born and a time to die. And all the years in between are under the watch care of God.

What is God saying to us through this Scripture? Even though there is order and routine, these seasons of life are taking place under God's caring eye. Because of His care, He is our comfort, strength, and our anchor. As you gather today, I point you to Him who can sustain you as you experience one of life's most difficult moments.

However, the verse to which I especially call your attention is not the one concerning a time to die. Instead, I encourage you to consider the wisdom of verses 5 and 6, particularly the reference to gathering and getting. The writer of Ecclesiastes reminded us that gathering up is one of life's experiences. "A time to get, and a time to lose" (KJV). Allow me to remind you—the family—that this moment is a time to gather up.

First, you should gather together your memory. Our memories are a gift from God. Although our memory should never be a hitching post to which we tie up and ignore present realities, we should cherish our memory of this dear one. Our memories of loved ones should never be anchors which hold back but sparks which move us forward.

The claiming of good memories is one force in life that motivates us and supports us through the good and bad of life. Your memory of this dear soul is a precious gift from God. Gather it up, and let it be for you a source of joy.

Second, you need to do some gathering of the present moment. Some difficult adjustments are being required of you. A special person has passed before us, and now there is the task of moving on. A part of this present task is the gathering of your inheritance. This inheritance may or may not consist of money. Money would be secondary to some things left behind that are much more important. Consider the inheritance of love given to you, and death does not negate the influence of that gift. Do not forget the name left for you. There is no shame or contempt, only pride in your name. Never take that for granted. We could produce a lengthy list of those gifts you have inherited. Gather them up and move from this present moment.

Third, this is a time to gather your faith. God is in this process. He has not abandoned you, nor is He punishing you by the pain you feel in this moment. Instead, He offers His strength, hope, and courage for your wounds. Now you must exercise your faith in Him. Claim your faith in Him as Lord of all of life, and that most especially includes the present moment. He cares for the one in whose memory we gather, and He cares for you. As you gather your faith, you will be able to move out of your grief and see God's hand at work.

Fourth, this day is also a time to gather your joy. This "Christ joy" is a peculiar one. An unbeliever cannot understand it. In the midst of pain and grief, there is joy in God's promise. It is the joy of knowing that death is not the end, only the beginning. Claim that joy. This joy is real; it is not a fabricated emotion.

The writer of Ecclesiastes has reminded us that life is not composed of one single emotion or activity. Life's experiences are varied. He reminds us that there is a time to be born and a time to die. But, especially in this setting, the opportunity is great to gather up. I encourage you to gather your memories, your joys, the present moment but, most of all, your faith. This moment is indeed a time to gather up.

Prayer: Gracious God, help us to see all of life's experiences as within Your control. There is rhythm to the natural order. Most of all, we are thankful that the routine and order does not rule out Your workings in our lives. Within Your order we have received and now give up this our friend. Bless the inheritance left behind by this dear soul but most of all the inheritance of the One in whose name we gather. Amen.

O. Finishing the Race
Text: 2 Timothy 4:6-8
Focus: 2 Timothy 4:7

In the text, Paul was writing to Timothy concerning this young man's ministry. Paul had now accumulated quite a few years, and many of those years had been very difficult. He was in a position to offer perspective on his own experience and Timothy's as well. Paul was primarily encouraging Timothy to do his duty. Timothy was charged to fulfill his ministry.

Timothy was reminded in the preceding verse by Paul that he was not a lone wayfarer who accounted only to himself for his journey of life. Instead, this young man lived in the sight of God who is both Observer and Judge. We are responsible to God for the stewardship of life. The way we use our days is of great interest to God.

Paul's age and circumstances add a moving tenderness to these words. This honest man of God had come to the close of his life and now looked back and used several images to convey his feelings. Moffatt translated verse 6, "My time to go has come." Death is not a great tragedy but simply the home going of one who has a clear conscience and the report of faithful service. The image Paul selected was one of the unmooring of a ship for a voyage overseas, "The time of my departure is at hand" (v. 6). While Paul never used the word, he certainly implied the term *victory* as he gave account of his days. Few verses in the Bible are quoted more often than this one in which Paul used the imagery of the games and made the claim that he had fought the fight. He had not only participated in the game, but he had finished what he began, and he did it without losing the faith. When he appears before the Judge, he will be crowned as the victor and given the wreath.

Paul's description of his own life is not boastful but an honest affirmation. In doing so Paul was reminding us all that life is a struggle. The race is not over until the finish line has been crossed. There can be no letting up until the game is done. There is nothing subtle in Paul's words as he suggested that we must not only start well but keep it up to the end. Indeed, keeping the faith becomes one of life's most difficult challenges. There are many rewards in life, but none compare to "the crown of a good life" (v. 8, Moffatt).

When Paul wrote these words he knew death could not be far away. Yet he was not afraid. He was as confident of God in death as in life. For him it was but a normal way to conclude a life of service. As a result of these words we may envision life from three perspectives.

First, there is life which is in the past. Paul said, "I have fought," "finished," and "kept." While he may have used the term *fight,* he was saying he gave it his best. He took life seriously—never took it for granted. He wasted very few minutes.

What a sense of joy one must have when one is able to look back on life and truly feel the best has been offered to our Lord. Paul appreciated life. After all, life is precious.

Yet notice that Paul referred to it as a "good fight." Why was it a *good* fight? Because his race was for God, and his faith kept him in the game. Paul said, "I have kept the faith." When our hour comes, will we be able to look back at our contest and say the same?

Second, Paul was referring to the life which now is. In his earthly state of mind, he was able to say, "I am now ready to be offered" (KJV). In other words my work is done, and now is the time to move on, a move I am ready to make. Only a man at peace with himself and God could make this kind of statement.

Paul is not the only one who could make that claim. We are mindful today that courage and peace are still possibilities. We have respect and admiration for the saint of God who can deal with life and death in this manner.

Third, Paul also pointed to the life to come. The apostle anticipated eternal life when he said, "Henceforth there is laid up for me a crown of righteousness" (v. 8, KJV). Most of us desire a crown, but do we really anticipate one? Christian hope requires both desire and expectation. Think of the difference that kind of attitude makes in our lives now.

There was no question in Paul's mind about his reward. Death was not a tyrant but a way to claim the life which was to come.

We have gathered here to honor one who has claimed the reward. The reward comes by way of a promise, and it is the same promise made to you and me. This one today has finished the race and claimed the crown. Yet remember that His crown is offered to all who "love his appearing" (v. 8*f*, KJV).

Therefore, in the midst of your pain and grief, there can be celebration. It is a celebration of life, life that is past, present, but most of all, life that is to come. May we all run the race in such a way that we too can say, "I have fought a good fight, I have finished my course, I have kept the faith" (v. 7, KJV).

Prayer: Lord, we realize that life is a race. As
            You observe and judge, give us

strength to run with faith. Most of all, for those who have run before us we offer our gratitude. Bless their memory as we follow their example toward the time. Amen.

P. Living in the Midst of Mystery
Text: John 13:1-7
Focus: John 13:7

The circumstances surrounding this passage include the washing of the feet of the disciples by Jesus. The foot washing took place before the Feast of the Passover. One can easily imagine that Jesus had so much to say to His disciples during this time. Surely He had so much He wanted to do. Yet He seemed to understand that these men were distracted and preoccupied. Rather than offer words which probably would not be heard, Jesus performed an act which was laden with significance. Scripture indicates that He got up from the meal, girded Himself with a towel, and began to wash the disciples' feet.

So much was happening to the disciples that they did not understand. There was so much talk about suffering, even death. They were being confronted with the reality that the kingdom of God was not what they had anticipated. Instead of their Leader and His group being raised to the ranks of prestige and power, they were being threatened with their very lives. Now just as they had learned to trust their Leader, He indicated to them that His hour had come to die.

The disciples found themselves in circumstances they did not understand. Things were happening all around them over which they seemed to have little control.

Now as Jesus began to kneel and wash their feet, they were stunned by the moment. The image presented is one of silence. The silence ended with Peter as this was more than he could stand. Surely, he must have been sitting in stunned amazement, like a man faced with some incredible happening. He gasped out, "Lord, are You washing my feet?" (v. 6). Jesus made a direct response to Peter's question about the washing of his feet. Yet Jesus' comment embraced the entire mood and setting when He said, "What I am doing you do not understand now, but you will know after this" (v. 7).

What does this passage have to do with a memorial setting such as this one? There are many things that happen to us in this life that we do not understand and for which we can

find few answers. Often in life we must be
content to live in the midst of mystery. Things
come upon us that do not look like love. From
where we are, these things made no sense at
all.

We may find ourselves having to face one
of life's most difficult challenges by learning
to trust Christ in the "dark," to accept His
ordering of our lives while remaining quiet in
the process. Just as Jesus knew of the confusion of His disciples, He understands our emotions as well. It helps in such times to be
assured that He knows how we feel, and that
He is not upset with us for those feelings.

He knows that it is not easy for us to grasp
why this dear one should be taken. Sometimes there seems to be no reason or purpose
in what has taken place. In the dark hour of
loss, sick with loneliness and anguish, our
hearts cry out for a reason and explanation. In
such times, we can find strength in the words
of Jesus spoken on the eve of His crucifixion
to His perplexed disciples in the upper room.

These words speak to you and me as we
confront life's heaviest loses. They apply to us
as we stand bereaved and mystified in events
for which we can find no answer. We find
comfort in the assurance that one day all that
now staggers us will come into focus.

There is a pattern being woven into the

fabric of our lives and, at this point, the pattern is not very clear. There will come a day when we all shall see clearly. Meanwhile, we must exercise our faith in Christ and trust Him in those moments when we cannot see. After all, has He not already proven Himself true and trustworthy?

As a minister I must stand too often before a heartbroken family. There is one reminder that I offer which may prove helpful to those who grieve. Beyond this difficult event, an event which defies our explanations, there is a purpose which faith alone can see within the shadows of the moment.

We live our lives in the presence of mystery. There are so many experiences we cannot understand. We are limited creatures, but we can be certain that this crushing blow is not blind fate, nor is it the result of an angry God. Obviously, all that comes our way is permitted by God, and only God totally understands the reason beneath all of life.

In 1833 John Henry Newman, in a moment of perplexity, wrote:

Lead, kindly Light! amid th' encircling gloom,
Lead Thou me on;
The night is dark, and I am far from home;
Lead Thou me on:

Keep Thou my feet; I do not ask to see
The distant scene—one step enough for
me.

So long thy power hath blest me, sure it
still
Will lead me on,
O'er moor and fen, o'er crag and torrent,
till
The night is gone;
And with the morn, those angel faces
smile,
Which I have loved long since, and lost
awhile.

In this kind of hour there is a question that comes again and again to our minds. The question is summed up in the word *why*. *Why* did this happen? *Why* has this person been taken from me?

Jesus knows well our dilemma. Out of the anguish of Calvary come the words, "My God, my God, why hast thou forsaken me?" (Matt. 27:46, KJV). In all of the Holy Scripture there is no verse more difficult to explain.

The Master was never closer to a suffering heart than at the moment of this outcry. Yet the final word from the cross may be our word as well. "Father, into thy hands I commend my spirit" (Luke 23:46, KJV)

Essentially, that is what we are called upon to do this day and especially this hour. We have gathered ourselves not just to commend the soul of this our departed friend, but to commend our own souls as well. In the midst of mystery the only option that makes sense is to commend our souls to the One who stands above and beyond all mysteries.

When life confronts us with mystery, we must at that moment place ourselves in the hands of One who does understand all that is beyond us. When the storms blow—and they will—we do have a source of strength and refuge. This stronghold cannot fail us. Our great defense is trust in the goodness and wisdom of God. "What I am doing you do not understand now, but you will know after this" (John 13:7).

Prayer: Give us grace to trust in Your wisdom which is above and beyond all mysteries. Teach us to rely upon You in moments of peace and when the unexplainable storms blow. Amen.

Q. The Mark of a Quality Life
(*For One Who Loved Well*)
Text: John 13:13-17,33-35
Focus: John 13:34

The Scripture verses selected for today's setting are very familiar, and yet, as a matter of practice, they are not frequently used in a funeral service. These verses, however, describe one characteristic of the Christian life which was embodied in the one in whose memory we gather here.

Consider the setting in which these words were spoken. The first verse of the chapter describes a contrast of moods. The season of the year called for a festive mood. The Passover was an important celebration among the Jewish people. However, the mood of those assembled in the upper room was very serious and heavy.

Jesus knew that the hour had come for Him to depart. Even for the Son of God, separation from loved ones must have been difficult. He loved all people, and especially deep was His affection for the group of disciples. The chances are good that He would have chosen to spend many years with them, but the call of the Father indicated otherwise.

Now Jesus had the task of leaving, which is

never an easy one. Surely, there were some very normal concerns in His mind. What would happen to them? After all, they would be facing a most difficult world. The world would put great pressures upon them as individuals and as a group. So much of their strength came from their unity. How could this unity be preserved?

Jesus taught them that only one bond would work: the bond of love. He described this bond as a new commandment. Yet, in one way, there was little new about it since this love bond had been perfectly personified in Him. The new commandment was to love as they had been loved by Him. This new commandment was very clear and simple. The disciples were to love each other as Jesus had loved them. This characteristic was to distinguish them from all other groups.

In the giving of this new commandment Jesus defined "disciple." If you were asked at this moment to define a Christian, what would be your response? I am sure there would be many different definitions. Hopefully, our definitions would reflect the qualification set forth by Jesus. We should love one another as He has loved us, and by this quality people recognize us as disciples. As we gather here to remember this departed friend, there should be no question in anyone's mind that we are remembering a disciple. Based on the words of Jesus this one easily falls into the company of disciples.

This world has many good people. In spite of our occasional pessimistic tendency to write people off, there still are lots of morally upright people. But Jesus is talking about much more than being morally upright. One can obey all laws and still not be found in the company of the disciples. The distinguishing mark is to love as Jesus has loved. That mark alone identifies the disciple.

As a memorial we can say many good things about this one today. So many of these characteristics are honorable. Yet nothing qualifies our friend more than the labeling as a disciple. This label does not come like an inherited characteristic of hair color, eye color, or body size. This label comes as a result of something one does.

In giving this new commandment Jesus explained what He requires of us. It is all gathered up in one word: *love.* We are to use our lives for other people and not just ourselves. What he desires from His followers is not that they should only do no evil but that they should do what is good. It is not enough that we hurt no one. More important is the matter of whom we have helped. One may keep the Ten Commandments and still fall short.

There is one additional command: "Thou shalt love." Human duty is summed up in the word *love.*

Christ becomes the measure against which we are tested. Therefore, the cross becomes our standard. Jesus did not say to us that we are only to follow His teaching. We are to follow His example also. Jesus has forever clarified what He wishes to be the distinguishing mark of His people. This mark differentiates the insiders from outsiders, believers from nonbelievers. This new commandment of mutual love becomes not just the bond that ties together but the principle witness to a lost world.

Jesus was deeply concerned about His special group of followers. Only the bond of love could keep them together. The same bond of love would distinguish them and become their calling card. In doing so, Jesus has defined the disciple.

We come together here for a number of reasons. We offer comfort to one another. We express our grief. We lift before us the banner of hope in Christ. But our gathering takes on special meaning because we celebrate one of God's people who made the mark.

Prayer: Our Father, we offer thanks for the undeniable characteristic of love in this one who has passed before us. May the bond of love truly characterize Your church and, most of all, our individual lives. Through Christ's strength and in whose name we pray. Amen.

R. Abiding Security
Text: Psalm 91
Focus: Psalm 91:2

Where can we find security and refuge in the painful moments of life? Is there something to undergird a soul in times of great loss? Only one fortress exists for such a time as now. Amid the hazards of our world we can find security only in the "shadow of the Almighty" (v. 1).

"If God is for us, who can be against us?" confessed Paul in Romans 8:31. He was experiencing an emotion very close to that of the psalmist who offered the exuberant song of faith found in Psalm 91. The confidence and hope of both men were rooted in God alone.

The psalmist observed many perils in his life. There was the hazard of the fowler's snare, the pit of destruction, and terror by night. Yet his mind was not caught up in these perils but in the security of the most High God. Asylum is found not in human defenses but in the shelter of God. He will be our refuge and fortress as He delivers us from all those things which seek to entrap us.

The psalmist painted a beautiful word picture of God's protection as a bird covering the young ones with feathers. It is an image of warmth and peace.

Humanity needs to have hope in something beyond our time and place. We must have hope. Hope is that which allows us to carry on with dignity. In this setting today, we need hope. In the midst of grief, we need a vision that goes beyond the moment. Yet we have an advantage over the psalmist because we are on this side of the Christ event.

God has given us that hope in the resurrection of Jesus Christ from the dead. Our Lord taught in the simplest language the reality of a future life. John's Gospel reminds us, "In my Father's house are many mansions; . . . I go to prepare a place for you" (John 14:2).

We who are here today are sure that death is not an end, nor does it leave one unclothed, but clad in an immortal spiritual body. We come together today to collectively acknowledge and claim the promise that life is but a preparation for a bigger and better life to follow.

We place our beliefs upon the authority of Christ Himself. The chances are that many questions were asked Him concerning the future. Yet, as one considers the teachings of Jesus as a whole, He said very little about the future life. At least He did not go to great lengths to explain the details of the future life. Instead, He apparently took the future life for granted. The answers He offered were very simple.

Basic to His understanding was the fact that "God is not the God of the dead, but of the living" (Matt. 22:32). We are also reminded, "Eye has not seen, nor ear heard,/Nor have entered into the heart of man/The things which God has prepared for/those who love Him" (1 Cor. 2:9). Our life on this earth is only a beginning.

If only we could take upon us the attitude of Jesus concerning death! He apparently took for granted that death is only a turn in the road of life eternal. Death is not equal to a dead-end road. With God being who He is, death just could not be otherwise. "In my Father's house are many mansions," Jesus said, and then very quietly added, "if it were not so, I would have told you." The essence of our Lord's teaching is that we should trust God. If we can trust God in this life, certainly we can trust Him in the life to come. Life is secure because of the character of God. And once we envision God as Jesus described Him, we are not afraid to make the leap of faith which accepts life and death without question.

Hear the consoling words of Psalm 91, "For He shall give His angels charge over you,/To keep you in all your ways" (v. 11). We are secure in all of life's changes. We live in a world where things are constantly changing. Things all around us are undergoing transition. Our world is just not the same as it was a few years ago. Our communities are not the same. Our homes are changing. We as persons are not the same. The seasons come, and the seasons go. Change is a natural part of life.

However, our security is found in the God who never changes. As we daily proceed into the future, we are assured of God's love and presence which will meet us and greet us every day. Jesus said, "I am the resurrection and the life. He who believes in Me, though he may die, he shall live" (John 11:25). In other words, God's love for us never changes.

Once we become confident of God's love for us, it makes all the difference in the world as we face each day. Our trust in God's love for us is imperative as we move into those times when life becomes difficult.

Consider, for example, suffering. None of us can adequately explain why good people suffer and die. Suffering, like all things, must pass under the watchful eye of the Father. Although we cannot answer the why question, we can trust in God's love and His wisdom for us.

One of our great challenges in life is trusting in the goodness of God in spite of life's mysteries. We must have trust that God knows more about this world than we do. He knows more about our individual lives than we do. Therefore, we can trust in His love and wisdom, not just for answers but for strength and courage. In this very moment, our need is greater for strength and support than for answers. If you had all the answers, the circumstances of the moment would remain the same.

The psalmist found security in the "Most High." Our security is to be found in the same Source. We are fooling ourselves to place our trust anywhere else.

So we gather here not to mourn the end of a life, but to celebrate the transition from one life to another. In this setting, there is always sadness and grief. These emotions are a legitimate response to loss.

Let us not forget that our primary reason for gathering here is to lift our eyes to a resurrected Lord who is our hope. In so doing, we claim the hope that death represents not the end of life but actually its beginning.

Prayer: O God, keep us that we may abide in Your shelter and in Your shadow. Give us courage to claim You as our fortress. You will deliver us in this moment as in all of life. Amen.

S. Christ Goes Before Us
Text: John 14:1-7
Focus: John 14:2

How could one find verses anywhere in the Bible more appropriate and meaningful for this time in our lives? So very difficult is the task of saying good-bye to someone special in our lives, but the invasion of death into our ranks forces us to do so. One psychologist has said that two of the earliest words a child learns are *hello* and *good-bye.* We spend most of our days moving back and forth between these two words. As intense as the pain of loss can be under the best of circumstance, our grief would be unbearable if death were a great dark chasm into which our loved ones fell and disappeared.

The comforting words of Jesus form a stark contrast to our worst fears of death. His first six words in the passage set the stage for what He is trying to accomplish: "Let not your heart be troubled." Jesus is calming the minds of His followers made anxious by His comments in John 13:33, "Little children, yet a little while I am with you" (KJV).

His word of advice and comfort to the disciples is that they should exercise faith—faith in God and faith in Him. "You believe in God, believe also in Me." Our Lord also directs His words to those of us gathered in a setting such as this, "Let not your heart be troubled." We need to hear those soothing words today just as much as those anxious disciples long ago. As Jesus observed His disciples, He saw them growing tired and weary. He is just as aware of your present circumstances.

There are some of you who have paid the price of exhaustion in the past few hours. Just as surely as to those disciples He says to you, "Let not your heart be troubled." These are not hollow words. They are a promise to each one of us.

Those early disciples had plenty to trouble them. Jesus was constantly talking about His mysterious departure. He was going away.

But where? In their hearts they must have known that death was involved somewhere along the way. Given the circumstances within and without, there was so much to cause great concern.

Yet Christ told them—faced by all of these facts—not to worry. Fortunately for their sakes and ours, He explained to them why they had no cause for great alarm. We need to hear His word of hope just now.

First, we need not be troubled. That is a rallying cry needed in this anxious world. The image rendered in the passage is that of an anxious mind. Fear can dictate our lives. We are always afraid that the worst will come. Christ would say that, even if it does, you still have no reason to fear. He verified His personal beliefs with His own life. Because He really did believe in God and did believe that God means what He says, Jesus was able to face the worst that life could offer.

Why should we not be troubled? Jesus said, "Believe in God." This belief means never having to manage on one's own. We can always go to Him and be helped by Him. We are to believe in Him as One to whom we have already turned many times and found to be true.

Second, death most certainly should not be our ultimate fear. Death is not falling into an endless chasm. Death for the believer translates into heaven. While we know very few details, the New Testament leaves no question that it is a glorious place.

Jesus knows our anxiety at this point. Whenever we are to take a trip, there is always some concern over preparations. When I arrive, will I have been expected? Will accomodations be in order? Jesus said with absolute assurance that preparations have been made. Each believer has his or her own personal and exclusive place in the Father's future plans.

Jesus made His claim in total trust of the Father. And He turned as though it were a subtle afterthought and said, "If it were not so, I would have told you" (KJV). Consider once again the image that is offered. When a special guest is coming to visit, we will make certain that everything is in order. We will know of those things which are special to our guest. The right books, food, and flowers will be appropriately placed. These preparations will be well thought out.

Preparations have been made for each one of us. Our coming and home going in life is no accident; therefore, God has planned well for His family.

Third, these preparations have not been left to chance. Christ has taken it upon Himself to make the arrangements. We are important enough that the Son of God Himself has taken care of our ultimate needs. When we encounter death, we do not embark alone. Death does not take us by the hand. Instead, Jesus takes our hand and leads us through a path He has already traveled.

Once again, we would benefit ourselves by claiming our trust in God. If we can trust Him in this life, we can trust Him in the life to come. There is no need for fear now or later on. Why? Because Christ has gone before us and made all the necessary arrangments. This claim is not the result of vague, wishful thinking. God's Word has established this promise for all people in all ages to come. Indeed, Christ goes before us.

And so, calmly and quietly, we note the home going of one who is known and loved. With courage and determination we move away from this hour to accept the responsibilities of those unlived days before us with full assurance that our loved one has only claimed the place prepared by the Lord of life.

Prayer: Our Father, we thank You that death is not the swallowing up of ourselves or our loved ones. We offer praise and gratitude for the preparations made for each one of us. Help us today to exercise our trust in You now and in the life to come. Amen.

T. Life After Death
Text: Job 14:14

How do we deal with death? In regard to our own deaths and the death of our loved ones, we must have some type of strategy for dealing with the inevitable.

For some the strategy is denial. The denial does not take place on the level of intellect. Only a small child could intellectually deny the inevitability of death. Our bodies and the world around us are a constant reminder that sooner or later time runs out for us.

The denial for most persons takes place on an emotional level whereby anything relating to death is simply pushed from our conscious minds. On a functional level the approach is "do not think about death, and it will go away." Yet deep within, we know that death is a reality, and all the denying in the world will not do away with it.

The believer and follower of Christ has a distinct advantage if one will let Holy Scripture guide one's thinking. The Bible offers a strategy for dealing with death which cuts right through the horror of death and describes this apparent enemy in different terms.

The horror comes when we envision death as the end of life, the termination of existence. There is no question of why death is seen as the supreme horror when understood as one's ultimate termination. The Bible states profoundly that death is not to be understood in such terms. The horror is removed when the truth is proclaimed that life goes on. Eternal life is not a fabricated human concept to ease the stress of life's termination. Eternal life is a reality being finally and forever verified by the death, burial, and resurrection of Jesus.

The biblical concept of death adds an entirely different dimension to life. Life can be approached altogether differently when death is seen through the eyes of our faith.

Job asked a question long ago, "If a man dies, shall he live again?" He was dealing with more than just a question of life beyond death. It was the certainty of the unbroken relationships beyond death of God and humans which offered hope to this despondent man. Job implied that if he could only believe what he truly longed to believe, he could then deal with anything regardless of how difficult it might be. Even Job's present suffering could have been seen differently if he had known that life could not be broken by anything less than the power of the Almighty.[1]

True wisdom makes room for the strategy of faith. Through our faith in God, we no longer need to deny death but to accept it only as a mysterious transition from this existence to life eternal. We, indeed, want to believe what we yearn to believe. The evidence for our case comes from God's Word and the life of our Lord.

Crito asked Socrates—after Socrates had taken the cup of poison—what disposition should be made of his body after death? Socrates answered, "You may bury me if you can catch me."[2] By his answer, Socrates revealed an intellectual faith in immortality far beyond his time. Job, too, had to deal with the question without the evidences you and I enjoy. The question of whether a person shall live again has been irrevocably answered in the life of Christ.

When God descended from heaven and took human form, we have our supreme hope for life now and life eternal. We have Jesus' personal assurance when He stated, "He that believeth in me, though he were dead, yet shall he live" (John 11:25, KJV).

The writer of Hebrews gave Christ the same position when stating, "Being made perfect, he became the author of eternal salvation unto all them that obey him" (Heb. 5:9, KJV). In the First Letter of John, the apostle stated, "We have seen it, and bear witness, and shew unto you that eternal life, which was with the Father, and was manifested unto us" (1 John 1:2, KJV).

There is for us today only one strategy that makes sense. Our approach to death must take into account the fact of eternal life. Our beliefs are not some vague, ethereal fabrication designed to make mortal life tolerable. Our hopes rest securely in the historical facts of the life, death, and resurrection of Christ Jesus.

Upon that promise of eternal life we can gather here in hope. Paul stated our hope perfectly:

> But I would not have you to be ignorant, brethren, concerning them which are asleep, that ye sorrow not, even as others which have no hope. For if we believe that Jesus died and rose again, even so them also which sleep in Jesus will God bring with him (1 Thess. 4:13-15, KJV).

Prayer: Our Father, for the promise of eternal life we offer our praise and gratitude. How difficult our lives would be today if we had no hope. But we do have a hope. We are called forth from this moment by the life of our Lord, in whose name we pray. Amen.

Notes

1. Nolan B. Harmon, ed., *The Interpreter's Bible*, III (New York: Abingdon Press, 1955), p. 1012.

2. Erdman, ed., *60 Funeral Messages* (Grand Rapids: Baker Book House, 1979), p. 66.

U. My Yoke Is Easy, and My Burden Is Light
Text: Matthew 11:27-30
Focus: Matthew 11:30

These were very difficult days for Jesus' disciples. They were trying very hard to understand life. Yet everytime they thought they had a handle on life, they discovered the unexpected. They wanted to be good followers, do the right things, and have proper attitudes; but life is at best, difficult. As you gather in this setting, you may be keenly aware of one of life's difficult moments.

Jesus offered beautiful words to His disciples as He said, "Come to Me, all you who labor and are heavy laden, and I will give you rest" (v. 28). He was speaking to people who knew well the experience of burdens. Some of them were farmers; some were shepherds; fishermen were present; and some may well have been slaves. Many of them knew very well the experience of backs bent low with burdens.

Implied in Jesus' statement is that burdens are common to all persons. The rich have burdens just like the poor. The high and mighty as well as the low and downtrodden have them. The old and the young alike are susceptible. No one is exempt from the common lot.

Your burden today is very real. The burden of grief is a very heavy one indeed. Yet we need to hear the words of Jesus at this point and to heed His advice. For when He invites us to bring to Him all of our burdens, the burden of grief is included as well.

To make a point, Jesus used a concept that was very familiar to the people of His day. Jesus said, "Take my yoke upon you, and learn of me" (KJV). Any Jew knew that *yoke* meant submission. They used the word with reference to the yoke of the law, the yoke of the Kingdom, and in other ways. To yoke oneself meant to submit.

Possibly, Jesus chose this concept because of something very close to His own experience. You will remember that Jesus was a carpenter, and the local carpenter was the one who fashioned the yokes for oxen. The yoke was made of wood and would be made to measure for a given ox. The assumption could be made that Jesus was an expert in making yokes that would fit well.

When Jesus said that His yoke was easy, He was drawing on His experience as a carpenter. He was more than capable of preparing a yoke that would fit well. It is such a beautiful image that He offers to us in all of life and especially in this setting.

He tells us to bring Him our burdens and take upon ourselves His yoke. His yoke will be easy, and our burdens will become light. None of our burdens are excluded from that invitation.

What does that invitation have to do with our grief? Everything! The burden you are experiencing now is certainly included in that invitation. The burden of grief is one of pain. Yet Jesus says to you this very moment to bring that burden to Him and place it before Him. He will take that heavy load and get up under the weight with you. He will give you strength to bear what you thought you could not stand.

As you deliver Him your burden of grief, you are promised rest, beautiful rest. He will give rest at its deepest level. In fact, He refers to it as "rest unto your souls" (KJV). How can one possibly ignore such an invitation?

All that is required of us is that we yoke yourselves to Him in our grief. To yoke to Him simply means that we submit to Him. How can Jesus help us otherwise? There is the promise that His yoke will be easy, and the burden will become light. How can we ignore the invitation of our Lord today? To accept that invitation can make the very difference between labor and rest, but only if we are willing to take His yoke upon us and to learn of Him.

Your pain in this moment is real. Pain is a part of life's burdensome task. We cannot avoid the burdens of life, but we do have a choice as to whether we carry them on the strength of our own backs or yoke ourselves to our Lord who has promised to get under the load with us and make our burdens light.

Prayer: God, give us the wisdom and courage to take Christ's yoke upon us
now as in all of our days. Amen.

V. The Need for Something Secure
Text: Job 1:2-3,13-19; 42:10
Focus: Job 42:10

We certainly do not have to live long to realize that life is full of uncertainties. Just as we think we understand life and can predict it, we are shocked into the reality that our knowledge of life is very limited.

Yet the seeming uncertainty of life does not mean that life is out of control. God is still over all and very much guides the lives and minds of all who so choose.

Such is the occasion of our gathering today. The fact that one has been taken from our company is not an indication that God has lost control. God, for reasons of His own, has chosen to call this friend home. God's taking this one is no less an act of love than choosing not to do so.

It is a date which all of us must meet. Some just approach it sooner than others. Not one of us is immune. That fact of life, of course, is predictable.

Yet we must have some perspective on life. We need an acceptance of its fluid nature— always changing. No one can debate that many of these changes are unpleasant and painful.

Job was all too familiar with this aspect of life. One day a messanger came to Job with the news that the Sabeans had raided the herds and had stolen the oxen and donkeys and also killed the servants who were tending them.

While this messenger was still speaking, another one approached and broke the news that a fire had "fallen from heaven" and burned up the sheep and servants who managed them.

Yet before this messenger had finished, another approached the stunned Job with the word that another group of his servants had been attacked by the Chaldeans who had killed them and had stolen all of Job's camels.

As if enough had not transpired in those few moments, a word came by another messenger that would tear at Job's heart. While his sons and daughters were eating and drinking in their oldest brother's house, a great wind came suddenly and destroyed the house (v. 19). The house had fallen upon Job's children, killing them all.

Unfortunately, Job's troubles did not end with these sad events. The Bible goes on to say that Satan caused painful boils to come upon Job's body from the crown of his head to the sole of his foot.

In just a matter of moments, Job's life had

been turned inside out. A life of joy and peace had been changed to a state of deep depression as Job endured what he had not expected or wanted.

Life is like that. At first it would appear that life's only certainty is change itself, with many of those changes filled with pain and distress. You find yourself in that position today. The death of a loved one produces mixed emotions. We trust in God's wisdom and power but that does not do away with the change we are thrust into.

Our experience does not have to be as extreme as that of Job to feel the need for something strong to grasp. In spite of his anguish and powerful emotions, Job never relinquished his faith. He never assumed that God had forfeited His control over life, especially Job's life. Job went straight to God with his concern, and rejection of God never became an option.

Instead, when Job could do little else, he managed to hold on to his deep-rooted faith and came out of it a stronger and wiser man. When his wisdom and patience came to their logical end, Job's faith took over and held on.

Your world right now may seem very unsteady. Change has invaded our lives again. The unpredictable has penetrated our ranks. Yet these painful times do not point to a God who has turned everything loose. A life is no more a victim of happenstance now than on the first day of creation.

God has not relinquished His power. He continues to be the unchanging element in all of life. When Job could do nothing else, he fell back on the unchanging nature of God. Job not only survived but came out a blessed man. The Bible indicates that "the Lord blessed the latter days of Job more than his beginning" (Job 42:12a). "So Job died, old and full of days" (Job 42:17).

In the midst of your pain and grief, there is a God who cares and understands. He offers peace for your turmoil. He grants strength for your weakness. Most of all, He offers unchanging power for a world that seems, at the moment, very insecure. There is a certainty to life greater than change. Our hope is the certainty of God.

Prayer: In these moments of uncertainty, give us grace to rest upon our faith. Deep within us we know the truth. You are the Truth. May these painful moments never blind us to the reality of Your certainty. In Christ's name we offer this prayer. Amen.

6
A Collection of Prayers and Benedictions

I.

O God, from whom all blessings flow, we come in great need of Your blessing. You and You alone know our broken hearts; You know the grief we experience. Out of our emptiness we come to You. Our reservoir of strength has been depleted; our souls are bare; our feelings are numb. Lord, we need You.

The seas of our life have been turbulent with sickness, pain, and separation. There have been times when we have cried out, "Why me?" We are filled with questions. We do not have the answers, so we come to You. Teach us to trust You, steady our faith so that in this darkness we may see Your light.

O God, grant that in all our grief we may turn to You. Grant us the peace of Your consolation and the joy of Your love. We ask this through Jesus Christ, our Lord. Amen.

Offered by: William Kitchen

II.

Father God, we come today as people whose lives have been abruptly changed by the death of one whom we deeply love. This change has brought confusion, anger, loneliness, fear, and doubt. In the midst of these varied emotions, we long for peace and for endurance. We want to feel Your presence.

As the stark reality of death is portrayed by this coffin and an open grave, may we remember that Your love is the ultimate reality. May we remember that the reality of Your love is stronger than death and now sustains life on a different plane for this one we love.

Lord, may the memories of precious moments shared sustain us in this time of grief. May those times of laughter and crying, joy and sorrow, energy and fatigue, conflict and peace which mark our history with this beloved individual be the foundation of hope which sends us into tomorrow.

Father, place us in Your strong resourceful hands, and do those things for us which we cannot do for ourselves. Amen.

Offered by: Branson Isley

III.

Our Heavenly Father, at a time when we are acutely aware of the death of a loved one, we thank You for Your living presence with us. Your unfailing companionship with us gives us comfort for today and courage for tomorrow.

In Your Son, Jesus Christ, You have revealed Yourself as a God of grace and glory. Through His life we have been blessed. Through His death we have been redeemed. Through His resurrection, we have been filled with vibrant hope.

In our sorrow, help us to look to the risen Christ. Help us to truly believe that what You did for Him You will also do for us. You raised Him from the dead to give Him eternal life. Remind us that You have promised eternal life to all who believe in You through faith in Your Son. On this difficult day, lead each of us to a deeper level of resurrection faith.

We thank You, O God, for our loved one whose life we honor and remember today. We are grateful for this one's vibrant faith, consistent witness through a godly life, and for a powerful influence upon family, friends, church, and community.

We pray especially for the grieving family.

May they feel Your comforting presence with them and know Your perfect peace within them. May they experience the reality of Your sustaining strength. May they realize our love for them and be encouraged through our prayers for them each day.

Today, we are reminded of the brevity of life. Help us to live each day with gratitude for Your blessings, with deep commitment to Jesus Christ, and with vibrant hope of eternal life through faith in Him.

This we pray in Jesus' name. Amen.

Offered by: Ronald F. Murray

IV.

Dear God of eternity, life is so precious to each of us that all that is within us says no to death. We see death as the dark, mysterious enemy that destroys the good that You have created.

Help us to see death as You see it: not the end but the beginning, not a wall but a doorway, not a dark road but a path that leads to eternal light and life.

We will miss our loved one, but we thank You, Lord, for memory. May our minds and hearts be filled with the wonderful recollections of the past.

Help our sadness to wear a smile as the

passing of time wipes the tears away. Time can be a great physician, healing the void that we now feel.

Every life is a gift from You, dear Father. Thank You for sharing this special person's life with us. We will cherish the memory forever. Amen.

Offered by: Rodger B. Murchison

V.

Our Father, for whom no dawn arises and no evening sun sets, we turn to Thee for light when our minds are dark and for strength when our days are long.

In these moments of sacred memory, we would give Thee honor for the life of our friend who has departed this life.

Make us content to leave this one to thy care, believing that Thy love for _____ is far greater than our own.

May light eternal shine upon this one. Thou art merciful. Grant unto _____ eternal rest, O Lord, and let perpetual light shine upon this soul. May this one rest in eternal peace.

And for this family, we pray that You will act from beneath, and hold them up. Act from within, and still their trembling spirits. Act from beyond, and affirm their hope—and ours. Cause us to hear again the direct speaking of our Lord as He said: "Come unto me, all ye that . . . are heavy laden, and I will give you rest."

Inspire us all with the thought that life is too strong for death, and that love never fails. Amen.

Offered by: Fred Moore

VI.

Dear Father in heaven, we thank You for giving us the privilege of knowing this dear man. We knew him as a Christian, a leader, a son, a husband, a father, and a friend. His love for You, dear God, was witnessed by each one of us, and that love was given to us by him. We miss him, but the warm memories we cherish remind us that he is now in Your tender care. Dear Shepherd, be with us in this valley. May your peace and comfort be felt by this good family. You are with us now, dear Lord, and as the psalmist said, "[We] will fear no evil" because You are here with us. In Christ's name we pray. Amen.

Offered by: Mike Watterson

VII.

Hear our prayer, O God, as we lay before You the concerns of our heart. Our hearts feel pain in these moments. Hear our cries, especially those that are deep and silent. You know the sorrow that has befallen us and You are aware of the grief within us. We come to You for healing and strength.

Lord, You have been our refuge for all generations. Men and women have called upon Your name since the beginning of time. Through this affliction draw our hearts closer to Your great heart of love. May these moments discipline us to train our eyes more steadfastly upon You.

We stand strong upon Your assurance that You have made preparations for us, in this life and in the life to come. Your loving assurance is our only refuge in this setting.

We thank You for the heritage of our faith. Through it our troubled hearts find rest even in sorrow. As we commend our loved ones to You, we do so with confidence that they rest securely in Your loving arms. Bless their passing and our memory of days which now appear to be gifts not only from them but from You as well. In Christ's name. Amen.

Suggested Benedictions

May almighty God, the Father, the Son, and the Holy Spirit, bless you and keep you, now and forevermore. Amen.

Unto whom, be glory and majesty, dominion and power, both now and forever. Amen. (see Jude 25)

Now may the God of peace Himself sanctify you completely; and may your whole spirit, soul and body be preserved blameless at the coming of our Lord Jesus Christ (1 Thess. 5:23).

Now may the God of peace who brought up our Lord Jesus from the dead, that great Shepherd of the sheep, through the blood of the everlasting covenant, make you complete in every good work to do His will, working in you what is well pleasing in His sight, through Jesus Christ, to whom be glory forever and ever. Amen. (Heb. 13:20-21).

Now to Him who is able to do exceedingly abundantly above all that we ask or think, according to the power that works in us, to Him be glory in the church by Christ Jesus throughout all ages, world without end. Amen (Eph. 3:20-21).

"The Lord bless you and keep you;
The Lord make His face shine
upon you,
And be gracious to you;
The Lord lift up His countenance
upon you,
And give you peace." (Num. 6:24-26)

The peace of God, which surpasses all understanding, will guard your hearts and minds through Christ Jesus (Phil. 4:7).

Now to the King eternal, immortal, invisible, to God who alone is wise, be honor and glory forever and ever. Amen (1 Tim. 1:17).

Now may our Lord Jesus Christ Himself, and our God and Father, who has loved us and given us everlasting consolation and good hope by grace, comfort your hearts and establish you in every good word and work (2 Thess. 2:16-17).

Now may the God of hope fill you with all joy and peace in believing, that you may abound in hope by the power of the Holy Spirit (Rom. 15:13).

May the God of all grace, who called us to His eternal glory by Christ Jesus, after you have suffered a while, perfect, establish, strengthen, and settle you (1 Pet. 5:10).

Suggestions
for Further Reading

Brooks, D. P. *Dealing with Death*. Nashville: Broadman Press, 1974.

Claypool, John. *Tracks of a Fellow Struggler*. Waco, Texas: Word, 1974.

Hudson, R. Lofton. *Persons in Crisis*. Nashville: Broadman Press, 1969.

Irion, Paul. *The Funeral: Vestige or Value*. Nashville: Abingdon Press, 1966.

Jackson, Edgar. *The Christian Funeral: Its Meaning, Its Purpose, and Its Modern Practice*. New York: Channel Press, 1966.

Johnson, L. D. *The Morning After Death*. Nashville: Broadman Press, 1978.

———. *Images of Eternity*. Marion Johnson, Compiler. Nashville: Broadman Press, 1984.

Klink, Thomas W. *Depth Perspectives in Pastoral Work*. Englewood Cliffs, New Jersey: Prentice Hall, 1965.

Madden, Myron C. *The Power to Bless*. Nashville: Broadman Press, 1970.

Oates, Wayne E. *The Christian Pastor.* Philadelphia: Westminster, 1961.

Sherrill, Lewis J. *The Struggle of the Soul.* New York: MacMillan, 1968.

Switzer, David K. *The Dynamics of Grief: Its Sources, Pain, and Healing.* New York: Abingdon, 1970.

Weatherhead, Leslie D. *Salute to a Sufferer.* New York: Abingdon, 1962.

AL CADENHEAD, JR.

Al Cadenhead, Jr. is pastor of The Hill Baptist Church, Augusta, Georgia. He is a graduate of Furman University (B.A.), and The Southern Baptist Theological Seminary (M.Div., D.Min.). He participated in Clinical Pastoral Education at Central State Hospital, Louisville, Kentucky, and Georgia Baptist Hospital, Atlanta, Georgia. He is a member of the American Association of Marriage and Family Therapy and is licensed by the State of Georgia as a family therapist.

He is married to the Former Mary Suzanne Lathem of Greenville, South Carolina. They have two children, Christian and Melody.